EFFECTIVE
MINISTRY

THE LEADER'S GUIDE TO
EFFECTIVE MINISTRY

How to face
the day-to-day
challenges
of ministry

WILLIAM WILLIMON

DALLAS WILLARD

LARRY BURKETT

MICHAEL SLAUGHTER | H.B. LONDON | DALE GALLOWAY
JESSE MIDDENDORF | NEIL WISEMAN | RON BLAKE | WAYNE SCHMIDT
JIM PETTITT | DARIUS SALTER | JEANNIE McCULLOUGH

Contents

Introduction

The rural house-calling physician of a bygone era presents a captivating image. At the bedside, during the long hours of anxious darkness he wiped the fevered brow, administered the potions and tonics and offered words of measured strength and promise to the family. When the patient's dawn of a new grip on life sent beams of hope over the horizon, with a handshake and a hug to those standing by – and a thanks to the Great Physician – the wearied 'minister of life and hope' emerged through the front door, black bag in hand; mounted his carriage; and disappeared into the sunrise.

The circuit-riding, house-calling minister of a prior generation traversed the back roads to sit in the evenings with the families of those who earned a more than honest wage – tilling the land, feeding the livestock and gathering the harvest. At the hearthside, he laughed heartily with them in their stories, joined in their harmonising round the upright piano, read the robust words of Holy Scripture from the family Bible, offered words of inspiration and counsel about the things that matter most, and talked with God as though He were right there – incarnate among them.

While every minister knows that these idyllic frames from the good old days offer somewhat romanticised views of those 'carers of physical health' and 'physicians of soul', the reality of the basic needs of life, including spiritual needs, has not changed. Even in our fast-paced, high-tech, 'instant messaging', electronic menu kind of times, the human spirit sends its age-old call, 'Please, I need the "realness" of person-to-person interaction, the warmth of spirit-to-spirit communion. Talk to me – talk to me as one real person to another. Talk to me about life, about the joy of relationships, about the significance of life, about some real-life connection to the Creator of it all. Tell me that life really does have deep meaning; that I can find an upper-level relationship with the One who made me; that in the whirl of making ends meet and navigating the murk and depravity of a sex-crazed culture, I can experience a life of purity, peace, and joy.'

I think you get the picture. You're on! You're the one! You're the woman – you're the man – God needs for just such times as ours. You're the one to minister anointed words of grace, of life, of hope. You're the one to help make the connection between despair and new life in the Saviour! You're the one who gets the 'front-row seat' to the transforming touch of a risen Christ in the life of a broken, lost, sin-laden soul. You get to play coach and cheerleader for the one who's been aching for something 'real' who then finds the One whose heart is longing to forgive, to redeem, to commune – to spend time with the 'comer'.

You're the one who gets to listen to the stories of broken relationships and offer words of Christlike wisdom and counsel. You're the one who gets to share the parental pain when the teenager makes a very wrong choice, but the powerful joy when that same young heart bows in contrition before the Redeemer. You're the one who experiences the grief, yet the celebration, at the bedside, when the sainted great-grandfather weakly waves goodbye and moments later peacefully breathes his last as he steps to a fairer land. You're the one who delivers the good news – before the congregation or beside an airline passenger – of a risen, redeeming Christ who, crowned with holy anointing, became one of us to 'bind up the broken-hearted, to proclaim freedom for the captives and release from darkness for the prisoners ... to comfort all who mourn, and provide for those who grieve ... to bestow on them a crown of beauty instead of ashes, the oil of gladness instead of mourning, and a garment of praise instead of a spirit of despair'. He came to make the redeemed ones 'oaks of righteousness, a planting of the LORD for the display of his splendor' (Isa. 61:1–3).

Because today's minister, equipped with PalmPilot, mobile phone and laptop finds parish ministry different – more complex and in some ways more demanding – than in yesteryears, he or she needs resources filled with wisdom, sound thinking and practical advice. *The Leader's Guide to Effective Ministry* was designed to be just such a resource. The veteran authors of this book address salient issues in the personal and professional lives of church leaders. Each essay addresses a vital topic – one the minister would appreciate hearing from this author over a conference lectern or discussing over a cup of coffee. Each author brings his or her distinctive personality, background, experience, ministry approach, and writing style to this book. Each addresses his or her subject by conveying angles and nuances unique to his or her own ministry. Thus the book takes on a life of its own through the spirit and style of each author as each one presents particular components of pastoral personal life or everyday ministry.

You will appreciate the real 'in the trenches' awarenesses and sensitivities expressed by these authors. They know ministry, and this expresses itself on these pages. They have written to encourage, inspire, challenge and come alongside you in your life of ministering to others. Allow God to minister to you through their writings. He has a vested interest in your being an effective minister of His grace, hope and life to longing souls. It is the prayer of the publisher that through these pages He will renew your passion for His call and make you an even better 'carer of souls' in your assignment.

THE LEADER'S PERSONAL LIFE

Dallas Willard, PhD, is a professor in the School of Philosophy at the University of Southern California in Los Angeles. He is a past director of the School of Philosophy and has received numerous academic honours. He is in demand as a speaker on spiritual formation. He has authored several books including *The Spirit of the Disciplines*, *Hearing God*, *The Divine Conspiracy* (selected as *Christianity Today's* 'Book of the Year' for 1999), and *Renovation of the Heart: Putting on the Character of Christ*. Dr Willard and his wife, Jane, have two children, John and Rebecca. The Willards live in Chatsworth, California.

Personal Soul Care

DALLAS WILLARD

Above all else, guard your heart,
for it is the wellspring of life.
Prov. 4:23

The call of God to minister the gospel is a high honour and a noble challenge. It carries with it unique opportunities as well as special burdens and dangers for members of the clergy as well as their families. These burdens can be fruitfully born, and the dangers triumphantly overcome. But that will not happen unless the minister's inner person (2 Cor. 4:16) is constantly renewed by accessing the riches of God and His kingdom in the inner person.

The Soul and the Great Commandment

'Soul' is here defined as the hidden or 'spiritual' side of the person. It includes an individual's thoughts and feelings, along with heart or will, with its intents and choices. It also includes an individual's bodily life and social relations, which, in their inner meaning and nature, are just as 'hidden' as the thoughts and feelings.

The secret to a strong, healthy and fruitful ministerial life lies in how we work *with* God in all of these dimensions. Together they make up the real person. They are the inescapable sources of our outward life, and they almost totally determine what effects, for good or ill, our ministerial activities will have. Natural gifts, external circumstances and special opportunities are of little significance. The good tree, Jesus said, 'bears good fruit' (Matt. 7:17). If we tend to the tree, the fruit will take care of itself.

The inner dimensions of life are what are referred to in the Great Commandment: '"Love the Lord your God with all your heart and with all your soul and with all your strength and with all your mind"; and, "Love your neighbour as yourself"' (Luke 10:27). This commandment does not so much tell us what we must do, as what we must cultivate in the care of our souls. This is true for all believers and is certainly true for ministers of the gospel.[1] Our high calling and sacrificial service can find adequate support only in a personality totally saturated with God's kind of love, *agape* (see 1 Cor. 13).

But we must be very clear that the great biblical passages on love – those cited above and others, including 1 John 4 – do *not* tell us to *act as if* we loved God with our whole beings, and our neighbours as ourselves. Such an attempt, without the love of God indwelling us, would be an impossible burden. We would become angry and hopeless – as, in fact, happens to many ministers and their families.

Character and the 'Fruit of the Spirit'

The 'sudden' failures that appear in the lives of some leaders are never really sudden but are the surfacing of long-standing deficiencies in 'the hidden person of the heart' (1 Pet. 3:4, NASB). Divine love permeating every part of our lives is, by contrast, a resource adequate to every condition of life and death, as 1 Corinthians 13 assures us. This love is, in the words of Jesus, 'a spring of water welling up to eternal life' (John 4:14). And from those possessed of divine love there truly flows 'streams of living water' to a thirsty world (see 7:38).

The people to whom we minister and speak will not recall 99 per cent of what we say to them. But they will never forget the kind of persons we are. This is true of influential ministers in my past. The quality of our souls will indelibly touch others for good or for ill. So we must never forget that the most important thing happening at any moment, in the midst of all our ministerial duties, is the kind of persons we are becoming.

God is greatly concerned with the quality of character we are building. The future He has planned for us will be built on the strength of character we forge by His grace. Intelligent, loving devotion to Christ will grow in importance through eternity and will never become obsolete.

It is God's intention that our lives should be a seamless manifestation of the fruit of the Spirit: 'love, joy, peace, patience, kindness, goodness, faithfulness, gentleness and self-control' (Gal. 5:22–23). He has made abundant provision for His indwelling our lives in the here and now. Appropriate attention to the care of our souls through His empowerment will yield this rich spiritual fruit and deliver us from the sad list of 'deeds of the flesh' (vv.19–21, NASB). We can be channels of the grace of the risen Christ, and through our ministerial activities – speaking, praying, healing, administering – He can minister to others. But we must attend to the means of His grace in practical and specific ways to experience His life into and through our lives.

'Practising the Presence of God'

The first and most basic thing we can and must do is to keep God before our minds. David knew this secret and wrote, 'I have set the Lord always before me. Because he is at my right hand, I shall not be shaken. Therefore my heart is glad and my tongue rejoices; my body also will rest secure' (Psa. 16:8–9).

This is *the* fundamental secret of caring for our souls. Our part in thus practising the presence of God is to direct and redirect our minds constantly to Him. In the early time of our 'practising' we may well be challenged by our burdensome habits of dwelling on things less than God. But these are habits – not the law of gravity – and can be broken. A new, grace-filled habit will replace the former ones as we take intentional steps towards keeping God before us. Soon our minds will return to God as the needle of a compass constantly returns to the north. If God is the great longing of our souls, He will become the pole star of our inward beings.[2]

Jesus Christ is, of course, the Door, the Light and the Way. We are privileged to walk in this profound reality, not just preach it. We first receive God into our minds by receiving Jesus. The way forward then lies in intentionally keeping the scenes and words of the New Testament Gospels before our minds, carefully reading and rereading them day by day. We revive them in word and imagination as we arise in the morning, move through the events of the day, and lie down at night. By this means we walk with Him moment by moment – the One who promised to be with us always.

As a beginning step in this 'practising' process, we can choose to practise constantly returning our minds to God in Christ on a given day. In the evening then we can review how we did and think of ways to do it better the next day. As we continue this practice, gently but persistently, we soon will find that the Person of Jesus and His beautiful words are 'automatically' occupying our minds instead of the clutter and noise of the world – even the church world.

Our concentration on Jesus will be strengthened by memorisation of great passages (*not* just verses) from Scripture. Passages such as Matthew 5–7, John 14–17, 1 Corinthians 13, and Colossians 3 are terrific 'soul growing' selections. This practice of memorising the Scriptures is more important than a daily quiet time, for as we fill our minds with these great passages and have them available for our meditation, 'quiet time' takes over the entirety of our lives.

God's word to Joshua, as he undertook the great task before him, was, 'Do not let this Book of the Law depart from your mouth; meditate on it day and night, so that you may be careful to do everything written in it.

Then you will be prosperous and successful' (Josh. 1:8). Psalm 1 demonstrates that this became a part of the recognised practice of spiritual living among the Israelites. Meditation on Him and His Word must become an integral part of our lives too.

But how does the law get *in your mouth?* By memorisation, of course. It becomes an essential part of how we think about everything else as we *dwell on it.* Then the things that come before us during the day come in the presence of God's illuminating Word. Light dwells within us and enables us to see the things of life in the right way. 'In Thy light we see light' (Psa. 36:9, NASB). This is the true education for ministry and for life.

Love and Worship

As the Living Word and the written Word occupy our minds we naturally – and supernaturally – come to love God more and more because we see, clearly and constantly, how lovely He is.

The wise Puritan, Thomas Watson, wrote:

The first fruit of love is *the musing of the mind upon God.* He who is in love, his thoughts are ever upon the object. He who loves God is ravished and transported with the contemplation of God. '*When I awake, I am still with thee*' (Psa. 139:18). The thoughts are as travellers in the mind. David's thoughts kept heaven-road. '*I am still with Thee.*' God is the treasure, and where the treasure is, there is the heart. By this we may test our love to God. What are our thoughts most upon? Can we say we are ravished with delight when we think on God? Have our thoughts got wings? Are they fled aloft? Do we contemplate Christ and glory? ... A sinner crowds God out of his thoughts. He never thinks of God, unless with horror, as the prisoner thinks of the judge.[3]

In this way we enter a *life*, not just *times*, of worship. The hymn of heaven will be a constant presence in our inner lives: 'To him who sits on the throne and to the Lamb be praise and honour and glory and power, for ever and ever' (Rev. 5:13).

Worship will become the constant undertone of our lives. It is the single most powerful force in completing and sustaining restoration of our whole beings to God. Nothing can inform, guide and sustain pervasive and radiant goodness in a person other than the true vision of God and the worship that spontaneously arises from it. Then the power of the indwelling Christ flows from us to others.

Remember, however, that we are not *trying* to worship. Worship is not another job we have to do. It is one aspect of the gift of 'living water' that springs 'up to eternal life' (John 4:14; 7:38, NASB). Our part is to turn our minds towards God and to attend to His graceful actions in our souls. This is the primary 'care of the soul' we must exercise. Then love and worship, worship and love, flow in our lives as we walk constantly with God. By stepping with Him – in the flow of His grace – we live with spontaneity, love our neighbours, and minister the word and power of the gospel.

Opening to the Fullness of Joy

Personal soul care also requires attending to our feelings. Emotions are a real component of life and of our lives in Christ. Some ministers allow their emotions to defeat them.

We do well to note, however, that *love* is the foundation of the spiritual life and *joy* is a key component in the Christ life. Joy is not pleasure, a mere sensation, but a pervasive and constant sense of wellbeing. Hope in the goodness of God is joy's indispensable support.

In a moment of worship and praise, Paul spontaneously expressed a benediction on the Christians in Rome: 'May the God of hope fill you with all joy and peace as you trust in him, so that you may overflow with hope by the power of the Holy Spirit' (Rom. 15:13). This verse addresses the profound needs of the emotional side of the Christian's life.

The great central terms of life in Christ are 'faith', 'hope', 'love', 'joy', and 'peace'. These are not *just* feelings; in substance, they are not feelings. They are conditions involving every part of an individual's life, including the body and the social context. They serve to equip us for the engagements of life. They do, however, have feelings that accompany them, and these positive feelings abundantly characterise those living in the presence of God. These feelings displace the bitter and angry feelings that characterise life 'in the flesh' – life in human energies only. They even transform the sickening emotional tones that permeate and largely govern the world around us – even many times the Church world.

Jesus taught us to abide in God's love '... that my joy may be in you and that your joy may be complete' (John 15:10–11). Our joy is full when there is no room for more. Abiding in God's love provides the unshakable source of joy, which is in turn the source of peace. All is based in the reality of God's grace and goodness.

Faith, hope, love, joy and *peace* – the 'magnificent five' – are inseparable from one another and reciprocally support each other. Try to imagine any one without the others!

Solitude and Silence

Among the practices that can help us attend to soul care at a basic level are *solitude* and *silence*. We practise these by finding ways to be alone and away from talk and noise. We rest, we observe, we 'smell the roses' – dare we say it? – we do *nothing*. This discipline can be used of God as a means of grace. In it we may even find another reminder of grace – that we are saved, justified by His redeeming power – not by our strivings and achievements.

In drawing aside for lengthy periods of time, we seek to rid ourselves of the 'corrosion' of soul that accrues from constant interaction with others and the world around us. In this place of quiet communion, we discover again that we *do* have souls, that we indeed have inner beings to be nurtured. Then we begin to experience again the presence of God in the inner sanctuary, speaking to and interacting with us. We understand anew that God will not compete for our attention. We must arrange time for our communion with Him as we draw aside in solitude and silence.

The psalmist said, 'Cease striving and know that I am God' (Psa. 46:10, NASB). And immediately following this, the writer affirms the success of God's mission on earth: ' "I will be exalted among the nations, I will be exalted in the earth." The LORD Almighty is with us; the God of Jacob is our fortress' (vv.10–11).

Other translations of this verse read, 'Be still, and know' (NIV) or 'Step out of the traffic! Take a long, loving look at me' (*The Message*). God's provision for us and for His work through us is adequate. We do not have to 'make it happen'. We must stop shouldering the burdens of 'outcomes'. These are safely in His hands. Someone insightfully said, 'The greatest threat to devotion to Christ is service for Christ.'

What a paradox! This is so easily a challenge for many ministers. Allowing service for Christ to steal our devotion to Him is a radical failure in personal soul care. But it is one from which the practice of communing with Christ in times of solitude and silence can deliver us.

Time Is Made, Not 'Found'

A response to giving attention to personal soul care often is, 'I don't have time for extensive solitude and silence. I have too much to do.' The truth is you don't have time *not* to practise solitude and silence. No time is more profitably spent than that used to heighten the quality of an intimate walk with God. If we think otherwise, we have been badly educated. The real question is, 'Will we take time to do what is necessary for an abundant life and an abundant ministry, or will we try to "get by" without it?'

So a couple of words of counsel are appropriate for our attending to the inner life. First, God never gives anyone too much to do. We do that to ourselves or allow others to do it to us. We may be showing our lack of confidence in God's power and goodness, though it may be that our models and education have failed us. Second, the exercise of God's power in ministry never, by itself, amends character, and it rarely makes up for our own foolishness. God's power can be actively and wisely sought and received by us only as we seek to grow by grace into Christlikeness. Power *with* Christlike character is God's unbeatable combination of triumphant life in the kingdom of God on earth and forever. Power without Christ's character gives us our modern-day Sampsons and Sauls.

Knowing Christ through times away in solitude and silence will let our 'joy be complete' (see John 16:24). It will bring over us a pervasive sense of wellbeing, no matter what is happening around us. Hurry and the loneliness of leadership will be eliminated. We can allow the peace of God to sink deeply into our lives and extend through our relationships to others (see Matt. 10:12–13).

A young Christian who had been guided into the effective practice of solitude and silence had this to say:

The more I practice this discipline, the more I appreciate the strength of silence. The less I become skeptical and judgmental, the more I learn to accept the things I didn't like about others, and the more I accept them as uniquely created in the image of God. The less I talk, the fuller are words spoken at an appropriate time. The more I value others, the more I serve them in small ways, and the more I enjoy and celebrate my life. The more I celebrate, the more I realize that God has been giving me wonderful things in my life, and the less I worry about my future. I will accept and enjoy what God is continuously giving to me. I think I am beginning to really enjoy God.[4]

Experiencing God through the practice of connecting with Him via this discipline brings rich rewards.

Planning for Fullness of Life

Our discussion so far has been more illustrative than expository. Solitude and silence are absolutely basic in our responsibility to soul care. But they also open before us the whole area of *disciplines* for the spiritual life. It is vital for us to keep before us that there are tried and true ways we can pursue towards abundant life in Christ. These ways are often referred to as 'spiritual disciplines'.[5] We can and must incorporate these into our lives as completely reliable ways of personal soul care. There is no substitute for this.

A person could make a long list of such disciplines, drawing on the history of Christ's people. The list would certainly include fasting, which when rightly practised has incredible power for the transformation of character and for ministry. On this list would also be such practices as frugality, service, celebration, prayer (as a discipline), journalling, fellowship, accountability relationships, submission, confession and many others.

There is no such thing as a complete list of the disciplines. Any activity that is in our power and enables us to achieve by grace what we cannot achieve by direct effort is a discipline of the spiritual life.[6]

As we seek to know Christ by incorporating appropriate disciplines into our lives, we must keep in mind that they are not ways of earning merit. They also are not paths of suffering or self-torment. They are not heroic. They are not righteousness, but they are wisdom.

Once we learn that grace is not opposed to effort (action) – though it is opposed to earning (attitude) – the way is open for us to 'work out' all that is involved in our salvation, not only 'with fear and trembling' but also with the calm assurance that it is God who is at work in us to accomplish all of His goodwill (see Phil. 2:12–13).

When we have settled into a life of sensible disciplines with our ever-present Teacher, then Peter's admonition (2 Pet. 1:5–7) to add virtue to our faith, knowledge or understanding to our virtue, self-control to our knowledge, patience to our self-control, godliness to our patience, brotherly kindness to our godliness, and divine love (*agape*) to our brotherly kindness will prove to be a sensible plan for life. God will use this course of action to help others through our ministries as well.

'As long as you practice these things,' Peter continues (v.10, NASB), 'you will never stumble.' In our walk with God in Christ there will be provided to us, from 'his glorious riches' (see Phil. 4:19), sweetness and strength of character, profundity of insight and understanding, and abundance of power to manifest the glory of God in life and in ministry – no matter the circumstances! And 'you will receive a rich welcome into the eternal kingdom of our Lord and Saviour Jesus Christ' (2 Pet. 1:11).

Notes

1. For development of this point see my *Renovation of the Heart*, especially Chapter 2 (Colorado Springs: NavPress, 2002).
2. For some illustrations of how this works, see Frank Laubach, 'Letters of a Modern Mystic' and 'Game with Minutes', in *Frank C. Laubach: Man of Prayer* (Syracuse, N.Y.: Laubach Literacy International, 'New Readers Press', 1990).
3. Thomas Watson, *All Things for Good* (1663; reprint, Carlisle, Penn.: The Banner of Truth Trust, 1986), 74.

4. Quoted from Dallas Willard, *The Spirit of the Disciplines* (San Francisco: Harper and Row, 1988), 165.
5. For further discussion see Richard Foster, *Celebration of Discipline* (San Francisco: Harper and Row, 1978), as well as his *Streams of Living Water* (San Francisco: HarperSanFrancisco, 1998). See also Dallas Willard, *The Spirit of the Disciplines.*
6. See Foster, *Celebration of Discipline*, as well as Chapter 9 of my *The Spirit of the Disciplines*, for ways of listing and classifying many of the disciplines and for discussions of any particular ones.

For Further Reading

à Kempis, Thomas, *The Imitation of Christ*. Many editions available. Apart from the Bible itself, this is undoubtedly the more republished work in Christian history. Absolutely indispensable.

Baxter, Richard, *The Practical Works of Richard Baxter*. Grand Rapids: Baker Book House, 1981.

Bouyer, Louis, *A History of Christian Spirituality*. 3 vols. New York: Seabury Press, 1982.

De Sales, Francis, *Introduction to the Devout Life*. Garden City, N.Y.: Doubleday, 1957.

Finney, Charles, *Revival Lectures*. Old Tappan, N.J.: Fleming H. Revell Company, n.d.

Law, William, *A Serious Call to a Devout and Holy Life*. New York: Paulist Press, 1978 – and many other editions.

Murray, Andrew. Especially *Humility and Absolute Surrender*. Many editions.

Nouwen, Henri, *The Way of the Heart*. New York: Ballantine Books, 1981.

Jeannie McCullough is a pastor's wife, a mother, and a grandmother. Her life and ministry have taken her to Bethany, Oklahoma, where her husband, Melvin, is the senior pastor of Bethany First Church of the Nazarene. In 1986, she began the Women of the Word Bible study, now called Wisdom of the Word. This ministry grew quickly from a small group in her local church to a video and tape ministry that reaches thousands across the country as well as several mission fields. Jeannie is in demand as a speaker throughout North America, due not only to her humour and honesty but also to her unique insights and application of the Scriptures in daily living. In 1997 Jeannie was awarded an honorary doctorate from Southern Nazarene University.

Soul Care and Ministry Vitality

Perspective of a Pastor's Wife

JEANNIE McCULLOUGH

Have you ever noticed that when the family gets together at special times during the year, the same old stories find a way of being shared? You know, don't you, that they're part of the stuff that glues the generations together?

One such story is told about my first visit to Kansas City in January of 1945. I was just 3½ years old, and it was my dad's first General Board session after his election as a general superintendent. My mother had decided to brave the cold and the complexity of bundling up twin girls to attend the first evening meeting. Our general missions' director at the time was Dr C. Warren Jones, and I am told he had a very distinct facial expression that caught my eye. My dad noticed my intense interest and tried to reach me before I said anything, but he didn't quite make it. To his horror he heard me say, 'Do you smell something?'

Being a little hard of hearing, Dr Jones knelt down and patted my blond curls. He said, 'What is it, sweetie?'

I raised the volume a bit and said, 'Do you smell something?'

Just then my dad reached me, swept me up in his arms and, with great diplomacy, steered the conversation in another direction.

'Do you smell something?'

That reminds me of what Fyodor Dostoyevsky wrote: 'I wanted to be left alone in my mouse hole. The whiff of real life had overwhelmed me, and I couldn't breathe.' As a pastor's wife I have had a whiff of real life, and at times it has overwhelmed me to the point where I could not breathe and my home was a hole where the sign read if ever so faintly, 'Leave me alone'. I even find those times recorded in Scripture, where the whiff of real life has overwhelmed God's servant and home was a hole. And then God called in a still small voice. I am convinced that often in such moments God does call – He calls us to search the soul.

But for the leader's wife whose plate is stacked so high it is out of sight, it seems impossible to stop, slow down and search the soul. Yet our response will determine our spiritual survival or suicide.

When I was sick as a child (and God knows I wanted to be when there was a test at school), my mother would administer her own home test with immediate results. To determine if I was truly sick or just sick of school – she said there was a difference (it's a mum thing) – first she would kiss my forehead to see if I was hot. Then she'd look at my eyes for redness. Finally she would smell my breath. And that was the clincher. One whiff of a sick child's breath and you know that the child's ill.

Often God uses the whiff test in real life to reveal that the soul is sick. The most common cause of its illness is neglect. Douglas J. Rumford's book *SoulShaping* is a must for every soul searcher. In his book he has listed 10 symptoms of soul neglect. Stop now and take time to search the soul, asking the Holy Spirit's help in answering honestly these thought-provoking statements.

Take inventory. The 10 primary symptoms of soul neglect are on the 10-point scale, from 1 (Need ISC! i.e., Intensive Spiritual Care) to 5 (Getting Flabby) to 10 (Tip-Top Condition). Mark your self-assessment on the chart.

Inventory of Symptoms of Soul Neglect[1]
1. Low-grade 'depression fever'
This is a spiritual depression in which a person feeling fine in most other ways, feels distant and cut off from God. This depression is best described in terms of coldness and unresponsiveness to spiritual things. This low-grade fever can be described as when one's life is blue and blah. There may be activity, but there's no fire. Depression can arise from innumerable sources. It is one of the most common manifestations of soul dryness; usually connected with one or more of the other symptoms listed below.

Need ISC!				Getting Flabby				Tip-Top Condition	
1	2	3	4	5	6	7	8	9	10

2. Busy but bored

Boredom is a lack of meaning felt in all the activities we are doing. Henri Nouwen wrote that boredom is a sense of disconnectedness.

Need ISC!				Getting Flabby			Tip-Top Condition		
1	2	3	4	5	6	7	8	9	10

3. Loss of control over life's routine

This is when we are overwhelmed by the demands of our life and unable to keep all the fires that we've started fuelled. Routine is one of 'life's economies', for it is both a time-saver and an energy saver.

Need ISC!				Getting Flabby			Tip-Top Condition		
1	2	3	4	5	6	7	8	9	10

4. Loss of responsiveness to others

In time of soul neglect, our relationships often bear the strain. We find it difficult to be with people we used to enjoy. This soul loss is apparent when we just want to check out of feeling responsible to and for others. We are tired with what some have called 'compassion fatigue'.

Need ISC!				Getting Flabby			Tip-Top Condition		
1	2	3	4	5	6	7	8	9	10

5. Withdrawal from responsibility and leadership

This symptom of soul neglect is backing away from responsibilities, including leadership. When we see other people begin to resist, refuse or renege on their responsibilities, their soul is calling out for care. A person may be dropping the ball because his arms are absolutely loaded.

Need ISC!				Getting Flabby			Tip-Top Condition		
1	2	3	4	5	6	7	8	9	10

6. Preoccupation with projects of lesser importance

This is where we keep doing things, but we turn to those things that are less demanding. Lack of energy and motivation may be a signal that your inner life needs more attention.

Need ISC!				Getting Flabby			Tip-Top Condition		
1	2	3	4	5	6	7	8	9	10

7. Restlessness and dissatisfaction

The loss of spiritual contentment is a spiritual problem. If the soul is restless, it is a symptom of an unmet need.

Need ISC!				Getting Flabby			Tip-Top Condition		
1	2	3	4	5	6	7	8	9	10

8. A resurgence of unhealthy habits, diminished impulse control and diminished resistance to temptation

When our soul needs attention, we may try to satisfy the wrong appetite. We may misread the inner discomfort we feel and do exactly the opposite of what we really need to do.

Vulnerability to temptation is the fever of the soul, not the germ of the disease. The parched desire of soul drought makes us crave the closest 'relief', even if it is toxic. Falling into sin is abhorrent, but a genuine soul need usually lies beneath the sinful act. We need to focus not only on the sinful act but also on the heart cry behind it.

Need ISC!				Getting Flabby			Tip-Top Condition		
1	2	3	4	5	6	7	8	9	10

9. Guilt and shame

Guilt is pain to the soul; it indicates that something is wrong and must be attended to. Most of us get confused by not understanding that guilt is an indicator.

A second dimension to guilt is shame. Shame is that sense of lowered self-esteem that accompanies a thought, word or act that you believed was inappropriate. Guilt says, 'I did wrong.' Shame says, 'I am wrong.'

Need ISC!				Getting Flabby			Tip-Top Condition		
1	2	3	4	5	6	7	8	9	10

10. A hard heart

This is the most frightening symptom of soul neglect. We see it when we knowingly refuse to do what we know is right or are unwilling to stop doing what we know is wrong.

Need ISC!				Getting Flabby			Tip-Top Condition		
1	2	3	4	5	6	7	8	9	10

Did you see yourself? This might have been the most productive time you've spent in months. Remember this. Henri Nouwen wrote, 'Time given to inner renewal is never wasted. It is the fuel for the journey.'

And, oh, how easy it is for those of us who care for the souls of others to discover that we ourselves are malnourished and numb, running on fumes instead of fuel. Satan would love to make us believe that Sundays will sustain us, when in truth they could sink us if they are our main means of closely watching our souls. For us, Sundays are often a fast instead of a feast as we are pulled in a hundred different directions, making survival the main goal.

George Herbert has provided some high octane fuel in these words: 'Dress and undress thy soul. Mark the decay and growth of it; if with thy watch that too be down, then wind up both. Since we shall be most surely judged, make the accounts agree.'

I want to share three steps that have strengthened my soul.

STEP 1: SEARCH THE SOUL – 'Dress and Undress Thy Soul'

The psalmist wrote in the 139th psalm, verses 1–4:

> O LORD, you have searched me and you know me.
> You know when I sit and when I rise;
>   you perceive my thoughts from afar.
> You discern my going out and my lying down;
>   you are familiar with all my ways.

Before a word is on my tongue
  you know it completely, O LORD.

Search the Soul with the Help of Scripture. My most satisfying times spiritually have been deeply rooted in allowing God to 'search me and know me'. It's only then that I can truly see myself. John Calvin wrote, 'Without knowledge of self, there is no knowledge of God.' Thus the *Scriptures* become a valuable tool for searching the soul.

Kierkegaard wrote, 'The lie of the devil consists of this ... that he wishes to make man believe that he can live without God's Word.'

One sunny Sunday at dinner, my daughter-in-law Carol (a gift to our family) said to me, 'Can you tell me what you did to raise your children to be so passionate about the Word?'

'Hopefully,' I said, 'it was by example.'

Travelling back in time, I remembered one dreary day while we were living in Colorado Springs. It was a Monday and rainy, but I was up early to fix breakfast for Ginger and Chris. Being a little paranoid that in health class the teacher might ask what they had eaten for breakfast (wanting to show by example their lack of a well-balanced meal), I made bacon, scrambled eggs, toast, juice, and finished with a flair by placing a Flintstone vitamin beside each of their milks. Having passed that test with flying colours, I was feeling a bit tired. But that was too bad; I just had to get on with it, because what happens between breakfast and making a break for the car is not printable, bordering on parental abuse.

Dressed for success in my uniform (a robe), I made a mad dash for the back door. Jumping into the car, I drove the children to two separate schools. Having a sense of accomplishment, I slowly drove towards home. Pulling into the garage, I turned off the motor. It was so still and silent. That thought was not finished when Mel shouted to me, 'Did you get your Bible off the top of the car?'

'What!'

'Did you get your Bible off the top of the car?'

'No-o-o! What was my Bible doing on top of the car?'

'You left it in my car last night!'

Mel always likes to clean out the car before he goes into the house. This time he had removed my Bible and put it on the car top.

A mixture of anger and anxiety filled my body. Throwing the car in reverse, I laid rubber down the long driveway. Flinging it into drive, I started to retrace my tracks. There in the middle of Academy Boulevard, the busiest street in the Springs, lay my Bible. Braking hard, I jumped from the car and, holding up both hands, I got traffic to come to a screeching stop. Kneeling down, I grabbed my Bible, wrapped my arms around it and walked back to my car. I couldn't even move. His Word was wet and wrinkled, marked by tears and now by tyres, this Book that I had grown to love. I wondered, 'Could it still speak?' Arriving home (I don't remember getting there), I slowly walked to my bedroom, closed the door, flung myself on the bed and opened my Bible.

'Remember the word to Thy servant, in which Thou hast made me hope. This is my comfort in my affliction, that Thy word has revived me' (Psa. 119:49–50, NASB). Yes!

This pursuit to know and be known of God is my passion and the path on which you who are serious about searching the soul must walk.

Search the Soul with the Help of the Holy Spirit. I'm reminded also of the significance of the *Holy Spirit* in searching the soul. Paul wrote, 'For the (Holy) Spirit searches diligently, exploring and examining everything, even sounding the profound and bottomless things of God – the divine counsels and things hidden and beyond man's scrutiny' (1 Cor. 2:10, AMP).

Only the Holy Spirit can uncover the hurts that have hammered the soul, the disappointments that have diverted its attention to the unimportant and unprofitable, leaving us a form instead of a force. It has been then that His hands have held my soul in its most fragile state, slowly revealing, resourcing and restoring it to health.

Search the Soul with the Help of the Saints. In the process of searching my soul, I have found that *saints* in every generation have become the serendipity of this journey. I'm reminded of an incident that happened to my granddaughter, Miss Haley. She and her dad, Jeff, were having one of those cherished talks together, cuddling closely in their big leather chair. Jeff looked lovingly into her large blue eyes and said softly, 'Sweetie, you know Daddy just had a birthday, and now most of my life's behind me. But you have most of your life ahead of you.'

She seemed a bit puzzled as he gathered her in his strong arms and placed a gentle kiss on her forehead. Then brushing her snow-white hair away from her sun-kissed face, she said, 'Daddy, I'll be six soon. Then will I have a little of my life behind me?'

Saints are those who share a journey half spent, whose companionship with Christ has provided a well of truth to drink deeply from. Their message and mentoring have helped me to make sense of the 'mysteries' that often surround my walk, making it possible to 'name the moment' that seems so uniquely mine, only to discover that they had experienced the same and survived.

STEP 2: SCORE THE SOUL – 'Mark the Decay and Growth'

God has helped me score the soul through the means of *truth* and *confession*. The psalms point to this in the following verses:

> *Surely you desire truth in the inner parts;*
> *you teach me wisdom in the inmost place.*
>
> Psa. 51:6

> *Then I acknowledged my sin to you*
> *and did not cover up my iniquity.*
> *I said, 'I will confess my transgressions to the LORD' –*
> *and you forgave the guilt of my sin.*
>
> Psa. 32:5

God has used the Scriptures, His Spirit and the saints to till the soil of my soul. This preparation has allowed me access to my innermost being, where I can see both sides of me – the public and the private.

A mentor of mine was sharing with me a special visit she had with her three granddaughters.

As usual on such visits, the two older sisters were my constant companions – playing, walking, reading, eating, shopping, going, coming, whatever – we were together! Even in the privacy of my room when I wanted to dress, the older granddaughter was always there; quietly, yet curiously watching. Being a rather modest grandmother, I would turn my back to her to finish my dressing.

Several times, I dressed in the bathroom. Here she would come! A knock on the door with, 'Nana, may I come in?'

'Oh, just a minute, honey, I'm dressing. I'll be out soon.'

The last morning I was there, I had to get up very early to catch my plane. I was hurriedly dressing and guess what? I heard the patter of little feet coming down the hall. Into the room came the 5-year-old in her nightgown with eyes half open. She didn't say a word but sat down in her little rocking chair. She rocked and rocked and watched. I turned my back and finished dressing. Finally, I heard a sweet little voice emphatically say, 'Nana, you haven't let me see both sides of you all week!'

For the soul to stand naked before God is at the core of intimacy with Him. It is here that He provides a protective place where truth liberates the trapped soul and confession is its constant companion. It is here that we can safely show both sides. In trying to protect our privacy, we often shield the soul from the scrutinising eyes of the Spirit, sapping it of its stability and strength.

STEP 3: SUPPORT THE SOUL – 'If with Thy Watch That Too Be Down, Then Wind Up Both'

S   *Singing* supports the soul.
     Singing soaks the soul so that it can soar.

U   *Understanding* supports the soul.
     The more we know the soul, the more we understand the soul.

P   *Praying* supports the soul.
     Praying connects the soul to its Provider.

P   *Praising* supports the soul.
     Praising prepares the soul for God's possibilities.

O   *Obedience* supports the soul.
     Obedience is the oxygen of the soul.

R   *Reflection* supports the soul.
     Reflecting on Scripture reaps a rich reward. It replenishes the soul.

T   *Telling* supports the soul.
     Telling your soul's stories strengthens it while teaching and touching others.

Our Miss Haley came running through the front door on a hot summer day, breathlessly calling my name, 'Mimi, Mimi.'

'I'm in the kitchen, Haley.'

'You won't believe it! You know Rachel?'

'Yes.'

'You know her dog?'

'Yes ... well, not really.'

Gasping for air, her thoughts now faster than her words, 'Well, well ... they just found out what's wrong with her.'

'With Rachel?'

'No, her dog.'

Jumping on the ledge, her voice lowered to a whisper while her eyes filled with tears, and she told me this story: Colett, their tiny toy poodle, a family pet that was the kind you treat like a person and love like family, had been losing her fur by the handfuls. No one knew what was causing this phenomenon. She seemed fine in every other way – playing, eating and sleeping. Yet she had bare spots all over her little body. The family agreed that she needed to go to the vet. So piling into the car, they drove to his office, while Rachel held Colett's quivering body. After carefully examining her, they found the trouble. Someone had put a rubber band around her tiny ear and forgot it was there, cutting off her circulation. Rachel started crying because she happened to be that person. The vet carefully cut the rubber band and told the family he had no other choice but to amputate the ear.

Spiritually there are times when we know something's wrong, but what? We found 'fur' but are clueless to its cause. I've learned that this time is crucial. Immediate care is imperative, for without it, spiritual fatigue sets in (where we forget what God looks like). This spiritual amnesia wipes clean our miracles from memory. I am an Israelite, one who seeks after God, and Scripture has my picture. How often these people of God seem to experience lapses of their spiritual memory. To such people Isaiah spoke the words, 'God does not come and go. God lasts' (Isa. 40, *The Message*). Hide those words – and at the hint of 'falling fur', say them over and over until your spiritual memory returns, recalling that the soul that leans on God He will not desert.

Notes

1. Adapted from *SoulShaping* by Douglas J. Rumford, pp.12–32. Copyright 1996. Used by permission of Tyndale House Publishers, Inc. All rights reserved.

For Further Reading

Beumer, Jurgen, *Henry Nouwen: A Restless Seeking for God*. New York: Crossroad Publishing, 1997.

Evans, Debra, *Soul Satisfaction*. Wheaton, Ill.: Crossway Books, 2001.

Foster, Richard J., and James Bryan Smith, eds, *Devotional Classics*. San Francisco: HarperSanFrancisco, 1993.

Maturin, Basil W., *Christian Self-Mastery: How to Govern Your Thoughts, Discipline Your Will, and Achieve Balance in Your Spiritual Life* (Abridged). Manchester, N.H.: Sophia Institute Press, 2001.

Yancy, Phillip, *Soul Survivor: How My Faith Survived the Church*. New York: Doubleday, 2001.

Darius Salter, PhD, is professor of Christian preaching and pastoral theology at Nazarene Theological Seminary in Kansas City. For eight years he served as chairman of the Pastoral Studies Department at Western Evangelical Seminary in Portland, Oregon. He was the executive director of the Christian Holiness Association, an inter-denominational fellowship consisting of 17 denominations, 50 colleges and universities, and two missionary organisations, from 1979 to 1986. He is a sought-after speaker in spiritual life campaigns and camp meetings. His published works include *What Really Matters in Ministry: Profiling Pastoral Success in Flourishing Churches*, *American Evangelism: Its Theology and Practice*, and *Prophetical-Priestly Words: Biblical Identity for the 21st Century Pastor*. Dr Salter and his wife, Brenda, have four daughters: Heather, Heidi, Tabitha and Ashley. The Salters live in Lake Winnebago, Missouri.

Physical and Emotional Health

DARIUS SALTER

Why an essay on the physical and emotional health of the American clergy, a well-fed, well-paid vocation? The article would be far more appropriate if it addressed the stress of Martin Rinkhart, who in 1636 preached at 5,000 funerals because of the ongoing Thirty Years' War. What about the dilemma of the Methodist minister, John Dickens, who died because he remained in Philadelphia to pastor victims of the yellow fever in 1797? We moderns should review the weariness of Francis Asbury, the founder of American Methodism, who travelled approximately a quarter of million miles, between 1771 and 1816, with stark deprivation as his accommodations. Typical was 'a crowded log cabin twelve feet by ten agreeable, without cold and rain; and within, six adults, and as many children, one of which is all motion; the dogs, too, must sometimes be admitted.'[1] Then there was Walter Rauschenbusch, who ministered in the notorious Hell's Kitchen section of New York City. Not many of us would want to trade our suburban comfort with any of the above or with hundreds of our predecessors who have ministered God's flock under enormous physical and emotional stress.

Stock exchange traders sandwich an 8-hour day between a morning and evening 2-hour commute; tired mothers work 80-hour weeks (two jobs) as grocery cashiers suffering from carpal tunnel syndrome; a plumber works a 12-hour day on a malfunctioning sewage plant with the stench almost unbearable. To single out church leaders as a distinct and elite guild of martyrs within a nation of diligent workers would be a mistake.

However, the lack of distinction between the clergy and the rest of society may be one of the beginning clues to understanding why many ministers believe themselves to be on the verge of mental and physical collapse. But before we search for clues to health, we must ask ourselves, what is health? To prescribe an ideal life of diet, rest, exercise and emotional space offers a superficial analysis of 'wholeness' or lack of it. Often those persons who are most deprived are most fulfilled, those who are most exhausted are most energised, those who are most wounded are most healed, and those who are most defeated are most triumphant. Life is full of paradoxes that defy simple formulas and in particular defy imposing a personal philosophy of wholeness on someone else.

For the Christian to confidently proclaim that wholeness is found only by moving towards reality is to discover that wholeness is only experienced by integrating life's most defining maxim, as expressed by our Lord, '[He who saves] his life will lose it' (Mark 8:35). Reminding ministers in an article on emotional and physical health that a good shepherd lays down his or her life for the sheep may sound as incongruent as preaching the gospel on board a 'Christian cruise ship'. The story of the cross sounds extremely off-key as it echoes off the enclaves of our pampered existence.

Any beginning exploration of wholeness must begin with the honest confession that none of us are perfectly whole. We all live somewhere on a continuum defined by varying degrees of defence mechanisms that include sublimation, rationalisation, compensation, triumphalism and defensive thin-skinnedness. Hopefully leaders are not more ego deficient than those in other professions, though they do seem to be in the only vocation whose members attach honorary doctorates after their names. Of course who can say that such superficial compensation is any more sinister than the dark forces that drive one to put his or her family through a PhD course.

No, it is not that ministers have more dark crevices in their psyches than other similarly driven professions. Most of us have 'make something out of yourself, Son or Daughter' reverberating in our unconscious. Church leaders are hopefully not more neurotic than other professionals. However, when the pastor neurotically extends or protects his or her ego, this extension does excessive damage to the Body of Christ. Public presence, pulpit proclamation, intimate relationships, privy information, administrative power and spiritual authority act as detonators, if not divested of self-interest. The church is often a powder keg of deeply imbedded ideologies, entrenched theologies, protective ownership and wounded memories, not to mention the dysfunctionalism of every family who attends the church's gatherings. None of the above is written for the purpose of discrediting the church. Our Lord reminded us that the sick need a physician, not those who are well.

The 'cure of souls' demands that the spiritual physician breathe wholeness into the malignancy of human existence. If the minister is emotionally sick, his or her sickness compounds the dysfunctionalism of the church. 'Saving ourselves' is sparing ourselves spiritual and emotional examination that will detect destructive malignancies. Living as a non-anxious presence in the shadow of September 11, 2001, demands superhuman emotional and physical resilience. This is not to say that ministers are to transcend all fear and frailty. They are to demonstrate that a person can be anchored to the Rock, in a violent sea of fear and frailties, which include the obsessions, compulsions and anxieties that surge through that person's own soul. This orientation can only happen via the abiding presence of the Holy Spirit.

I may be forming the impression that I am more afraid of neurosis than hell itself. Allow me to be the first to admit that the world is a better place because Martin Luther had an overly stern father, John Wesley was singled out as a favourite by his mother and Francis Asbury was an only child. Yes, introspection, feeling one's pulse to find debilitating origins, is liable to the law of diminishing returns. But may I suggest with little hesitation that the American church pastored by spiritual or psychological hypochondriacs is not our greatest problem. Few of us have plumbed the depths of Bernard of Clairvaux's *Twelve Steps to Humility* or Ignatius's *Spiritual Exercises*. I write with a bit of sarcasm (a defence mechanism) that the above or similar routes to honesty and vulnerability are outdated in the fast-paced world of today's modern leader, armed with laptop and cell phone. Don't allow my antitechnology stance (does technology make us better soul physicians?) to preempt your labour-saving devices.

But please allow me to suggest that the pastor would be a better person and the church a more redemptive organism if he or she would replace one leadership seminar with several hours of gut-wrenching and soul-cleansing confession to a trusted spiritual adviser; if the latest how-to book was replaced with honest prostration before God; and if some ongoing denominational activity could be replaced by interdenominational prayer and fellowship among a small group of pastors from big and small churches who emphasise confession and repentance of the ugly sin of pride that stalks all of us, especially pastors.

Clearly, all of the above could depreciate either into a self-pity session or spiritual elitism. Thus all moves towards wholeness must be defined by the question, 'What is most redemptive for me so I can in turn be more redemptive to others?' High blood pressure caused by not recognising personal limitations, obesity caused by overeating and not exercising, and falling asleep in a counselling session because of watching late-night television can hardly bring glory to God and healing to those placed under our spiritual care.

The disciplines of theology offer growth for both soul and mind, and technology provides the means or at least some of the means to carry out the tasks prescribed by theology. But both theology and technology are slippery slopes. The betraying illusions of each misguide ministers into false assumptions of effectiveness and omnipresence. Ministers who are 'called by God', 'favoured by God', in need of impressing God and armed with the latest technology of travel and communication doubly jeopardise themselves and the people they serve. The unwillingness to recognise our limitations in a world that is exponentially ignoring time and space is undermining the unique identity of the minister as a person of contemplation in a hurry-up world.

Serving a supernatural God does not mean we can ignore the law of gravity. Human limitations demand that the minister differentiate God's requirements from the church's requirements, from the denomination's requirements and, most of all, from the requirements of self-adulation. A physician, Dan Spaite, accurately states, 'First, ministers must face the issues of personal choice. They must understand that the path of obedience requires prioritizing their too busy list according to God's approval. This must include all issues not just ministry ones.'[2] The secret to the wholeness of Jesus was His relationship to His Father. Jesus spent His life doing the will of the Father.

The plight of Francis Asbury was hardly singular. He was quite representative of the hundreds of Methodist itinerants (as well as Baptists) who tamed the frontier by enduring dire circumstances. The historical irony is that these men who modelled the martyr's life of poverty, chastity and obedience lived longer than the average population of the late eighteenth century. This cautions us against singling out church leadership as an overworked, burned-out profession. The problem for today's minister is not so much his or her uniqueness; it is nondifferentiation with the prevailing zeitgeist (spirit of the times). Ministers have not allowed God to mould them into the prophet/priests who question the world's definition of blessedness and model kingdom living. Kingdom dwellers exemplify that relationships are more important than accomplishments, community takes precedent over individualism, and families demand significant investment of time and energy if they are to become agents of construction rather than destruction.

The quest for physical and emotional wholeness is not found in formulas but in the mind of Christ. Sleep more, recreate more, exercise more, get away more – all may be helpful imperatives. But these suggestions may serve as mere self-help guides for a society taking its cues from the goddess Nike rather than the God Yahweh.

I do not deny that there are unique pressures on the minister: on call

24-7; on public display; on evening duty; and attempting to lead, pacify and placate people who often make unreasonable demands. And if ministers do not meet parishioners' demands, congregants may quickly seek out another pastor or church. The consumer index stalks a minister's emotional well-being perhaps more than any other enemy. Both pastoral demands that are a traditional part of the job description and pastoral challenges that are unique to the twenty-first century are to be discussed with spouse and children, analysed with peers and constantly offered up to the God who has called us. All of us need to know when we have crossed the line between doing good and doing harm. Doing harm in the name of Christian ministry is a pathology too often undetected. Doing God's will should never leave a path of spiritual and emotional destruction.

Above all people, ministers need to defy modernity's equating busyness with significance. Richard Swenson has defined 'margin' as having something left over after fulfilling the requirements of time, money and energy.[3] He makes a helpful point. We live in a society exhausting itself going nowhere other than broken relationships, destructive addictions and the suffocation of things. We fill every minute with something to do, and if there is a miscue in our day, we find ourselves in a state of panic. Isaiah penetratingly asked, 'Why do you spend money for what is not bread, and your wages for what does not satisfy?' (Isa. 55:2, NASB). But maintaining emotional and physical health (I think Swenson would agree) is not so much having something in reserve. The healthy person is the person who expends everything on the right thing. Mental and physical health is usually not improved by doing less or doing more. Wholeness is nurtured by doing what I ought to do, when I ought to do it, for the glory of God. This wisdom comes only from God.

Far more ministers impair themselves by relational blunders rather than by being overworked. Whatever words or actions increase healthy relationships with those closest to us, namely our immediate families, will promote our own welfare and the welfare of those to whom we minister. The leader who is not in right relationship with his or her spouse and children will not be in right relationship with his or her parishioners. Relationships are compounded and played out in ever-receding concentric circles. Pastoring demands such undivided focus (preaching, counselling, etc.) that domestic fragmentation in a minister's personal life contaminates ministry. Redemptive solvency is best offered by those who pay careful attention to their private accounts with God and others with whom they are most intimate.

A sense of wellbeing is critical if a minister is to extend Spirit-anointed means of grace to the crises and potentials of human existence. A sense of wellbeing is essential to wellbeing. The critical threat to this sense of wellbeing is a culture that equates effectiveness with measurement. The most important things ministers do cannot be measured. 'How many ounces of forgiveness did John receive?' and 'How many pounds of reconciliation took place between Sue and Mary?' are unanswerable because of ludicrous disjunctions. Unless the minister is willing to accept a countercultural job description propelled by the mysteries of grace, rather than success motifs, he or she will be plagued with an abiding disease. Pastoring is not a normative job.

The minister's psyche must bear the delicate perspective that all personal fulfillment must be sacrificed to God. Nothing that the minister has may be retained. At the same time, any attempts at achieving humility (or appearing humble) by masking inherent needs for significance, affirmation, acceptance and the esteem of others is harmful. Charles Rassieur states, 'So the identity of the pastor as it becomes visible in his pastoral care is born from the intangible tension between self-affirmation and self-denial, self-fulfillment and self-emptying, self-realisation and self-sacrifice.'[4]

Intentionality translates into security of identity, a sense that a person is controlling his or her own destiny. Or better yet, a person is able by the power of the Holy Spirit to allow God to shape his or her destiny rather than be blown about by conflicting cultural winds that constantly change direction. The healthy leader is not a weather vane but instead possesses a theological compass that provides direction for leadership. Without certitude of direction and identity, his or her time and energy become fragmented. Fragmentation is more detrimental to the leader's health than being overworked.

A dozen years ago, I polled 100 pastors whose church attendance averaged over 1,650 on Sunday morning. The time commitment of these pastors to their churches averaged 55 hours per week. In other words, they gave their employer the amount of time expected of any CEO. Today's ministers have all the time they need to spend with their families, play golf, hunt, fish or do whatever. For the most part, all of us lie when we say we do not have the time to exercise, pray and spend quality family time. More accurately, we should say when turning down an invitation to join an interdenominational sermon preparation session, 'I perceive other use of my time is in keeping with my value system.'

Conscientious pastoring does not have to produce regrets that I was not there for my daughter's basketball game or my son's recital. (But also let me insert that good parenting can take place without attending every sports event and every recital.) According to James Glasse, a pastor puts in

30 to 40 hours per week in order to 'pay the rent' in his or her church.[5] Any time beyond that becomes discretionary time or creative time. Creative time fuels energy. If a minister's time is totally consumed by doing what he or she has to do, stagnation sets in, and meaninglessness is the result. This malaise of spirit is the sure route to emotional and physical breakdown.

Blurring quality-self with quantity-self creates confusion for the minister. My wife would rather have two hours given to her by an energetic husband than by a worn-out distracted husband. As leaders we are not called to be ourselves when we stand in the pulpit or counsel a parishioner; we are called to be our best selves. Twenty minutes of insight energised by physical and emotional alertness are worth more to a congregation individually or corporately than several hours of haggard engagement.

Every vocation is liable to unique occupational hazards. Allow me to suggest a few that represent emotional/physical detriments for the minister.

The Sunday Work Syndrome

I observe the minister as the most likely person to neglect God's provision for one day of rest and recreation out of every seven. Keeping the Sabbath is God's design for continuing His creation in us (re-creation) and saving us from self-destruction. Restlessness is a pervasive disease that causes its victims to believe that the essence of life is doing. Few of us possess the theological confidence of Martin Luther, who stated, 'While I drink my little glass of Wittenberg beer, the gospel runs its course.' Weariness is worn as a badge of honour, busyness is touted as a sign of importance, and 'I am needed 24-7' is a defence mechanism that produces pseudo significance.

Sunday is an exhausting day. The minister often utilises Monday as his or her Sabbath. However, the minister is so depleted on Monday that any meaningful recreation or rejuvenation through focusing on God and family is almost impossible. I tend to agree with Eugene Peterson that Sabbath is other and more than a 'day off'. The Sabbath is a day devoted to playing and praying, activities that demand energy, investments with critical returns, emotionally and physically. The Sabbath is a means of grace, a gift from God that allows us to 'separate ourselves from the people who are clinging to us, from the routines to which we are clinging for our identity, and offering them all up to God in praise.'[6]

The Western minister needs to be mindful that he or she is ministering to 'restless, greedy children of disproportion; caught in an idolizing of acquisitiveness'.[7] God instituted the Hebrew Sabbath to save us from our cannibalising selves. The Sabbath is an act of trust that recognises blessedness as other than acquiring and doing. The minister is to model a rhythm that discounts communion with that which cannot commune, possessions. God's own seventh-day rest stated that 'the world is not marked by frenzy, precariousness, threat, or restlessness. God's sovereignty is so sure that even God can ease off daily management of creation and the world will not fall apart.'[8] And neither will the Church.

The Church-Life Syndrome

Church organisation is far more complex today than it was 50 years ago. Every church is a megachurch or thinks it ought to be one. Thus the life of the organism evolves into organisational complexity. The local church assumes a life of its own; that is, it becomes an end in itself. We have assumed that quality of spiritual life is equivalent to a frenzy of activities. In the minds of both parishioner and the pastoral family, the life of the local church is equated with the kingdom of God. The minister and his or her family perceive themselves as models of commitment to the church and its activities, lest any of the flock fall short. This exhausting routine cuts into meaningful communication, worship and recreation with significant others for whom God has given us explicit responsibility for maturation, in particular, our immediate families. One 40-year-old PhD sat down with his hard-working pastoral dad, now retired. They both wept together as the son stated, 'Dad, you weren't there when I needed you.'

But there is even a more critical problem than nonavailability to significant others because of long workdays. Constant church activity becomes equated with genuine Christianity. If church life represents in the minds of children the totality of what Christianity means, then when the church fails, Christianity has failed. All churches fail to fully represent God's kingdom on earth. The result is disillusionment with both God and the church by the leader and his or her family. If church and God are synonymous, then a defect in the former is a defect in the latter.

May I suggest that the minister's family needs to be involved in activities outside the church: scouts, Philharmonic orchestra, athletics or whatever is in keeping with their aptitude. Thus spirituality becomes holistic and the family is enabled to integrate Christianity with the various facets of life. This extramural involvement allows for meaningful communication about what it means to be Christian in a pagan world. Activity in the world permits integration, a defining motif for all of life that is consistent and noncompartmentalised. Kingdom living, which allows for a highly differentiated self in a world that is no friend to grace, fosters inner security that God alone can provide. The leader and his or her family need to be involved in activities beyond the cloister that allow them to participate in God's kingdom on earth.

The Persona Syndrome

For 1900 years, introverted individuals fulfilled the mandates of pastoring that included study, prayer, spiritual direction, contemplation and other disciplines of the inner life. Being God-oriented, to the extent that one hears the 'call of God', is compatible with introversion and disengagement from people.

With the age of industrialisation, which consists of the technology of automation, persons found themselves interacting with things rather than people. Placing the same bolt in the same place on a thousand engines per day produced meaninglessness. No one better captured this than Joe Glazer in 'You Gotta Fight That Line':

> *They put me to work on the assembly line,*
> *My clock-card number was 90-90-9.*
> *Those Fords rolled by on that factory floor,*
> *And every fourteen seconds I slapped on a door.*
> *Those Fords rolled by all day and all night,*
> *My job was the front door on the right.*
> *Foreman told me the day I was hired,*
> *'You miss one door, Mr. Jones ... you're fired.'*
> *I slapped those doors on, always on the run,*
> *Every fourteen seconds, never missed a one.*
> *And I staggered home from work each night,*
> *Still slappin' em on – front door right.*

There are millions of persons in the West who daily interact with things – computer screens, paper, car parts and so on – rather than people. The emotional stability provided by relationships characteristic to small communities has been eroded by industrialisation, urbanisation, television and various other obstacles that prevent incarnational engagement. The church has always been a place that bonds people together. But in the past, this bonding was supplemented by the hegemony of secular communities that fostered relationships.

Now that persons live out their lives electronically, high-tech demands 'high touch'. And the minister is expected to be the chief of high touch. For the present generation of churchgoers, the most important quality of the leader is his or her relational skills, which may be stated simply as friendliness. In other words, for consumers, the ability of the minister to glad hand is often more important than theological integrity or preaching ability. In a day marked by personality cults, it is not unusual for a leader to plant a church, increase its attendance to 500 over a 5-year period, and then watch it go out of business when he or she leaves.

Leaders who are not naturally extroverted find putting up a front with the right countenance for everyone they meet emotionally exhausting. I well remember the sigh I would breathe after I greeted the last postservice person as he or she filed out the door Sunday morning. The tension between one's persona and one's real self creates overbearing stress resulting in headaches, backaches, fatigue and a hundred other symptoms. Those leaders who find energy from introversion must make sure there is sufficient time given to activities that feed their emotional energy rather than drain it. There is a fine line between possessing enough psychic space to absorb people and their problems and being enslaved to them. Jesus' 'slipping away' to the Mount of Olives prototypes the perfect model for maintaining temperamental balance. The minister must get away.

Problem Intake Syndrome

Pastors continue to carry a large portion of the counselling load. Individuals come to ministers to find a listening ear. The role of pastoral counselling is ensured by the hope that the pastor has a 'word from God'. The pastor serves as an authority figure who elicits unconditional positive regard and invites catharsis for guilt or other psychological trauma. Thus during the course of the day he or she may hear the sobbing story of a father addicted to pornography, of a young lady molested by someone in her past, or of a couple whose home is breaking up, and an almost endless list of problems endemic to a society failing at relationships.

What does a pastor do with that kind of intake? Is there someone with whom he or she can share and who, in turn, will enable him or her to experience catharsis (cleansing) rather than repression? Is there a ritual in spoken or active word that releases the pastor from the accumulated burden that accretes around the soul? Perhaps the pastor should symbolically wash his or her hands or even anoint himself or herself with oil at the end of the day. Is there a prayer the pastor can pray that transforms him or her into a courier, one who delivers the burden of his or her people to God?

'Lord, I release this day to You with all of its events. Thank You for the opportunity to minister to [person's name]. His [or her] answer is not found in me but in You. I must decrease, and You must increase. May Your Spirit continue to pray through me, even beyond my consciousness. Enable me to rest in the fact that Christ is praying for this situation and the ultimate answer for this situation is Christ's healing love. May Christ's grace place closure on this day and cleanse away any residue that would leave an ugly stain on my mind and body. I enter into nocturnal rest with the knowledge that my body is the temple of the Holy Spirit. I pray this in the name of the Father and of the Son and of the Holy Spirit. Amen.'

The Praise-Blame Syndrome

No professionals in the United States receive more verbal affirmation than pastors or church leaders. Any given leader may hear 'good sermon' 100 or more times on Sunday morning, not to mention the 'thank you' notes for weddings and funerals. The leader is also susceptible to an onslaught of criticism. For anything that goes wrong, he or she is the most visible lightning rod. I suspect that the leader most inflated by praise is most deflated by criticism. Taking both with a grain of salt is a sign of maturity. Failure for us to find emotional bearings from God, the one constant in our lives, exposes us to the fickleness of both supporters and detractors.

Constancy, consistency and commitment in ministry are enhanced by ego divestment – the attitude that God's cause is at stake, not mine. When my popularity and success are the main items for accentuation and preservation, any dent in their enhancement leads to anxiety. Maintaining a non-anxious presence in the pastorate is the pastor's only mode for living within healthy parameters for both mind and body. The only completely whole person whoever walked this earth was crucified. For the 21st-century Western leader, death is the only route to life.

Notes

1. Francis Asbury, *Journal and Letters*, ed. Elmer Clark, J. Manning Potts, and Jacob S. Payton, vol. 2 (London: Epworth Press, 1958), 410–11.
2. Daniel Spaite, *Time Bomb in the Church: Defusing Pastoral Burnout* (Kansas City: Beacon Hill Press of Kansas City, 1999), 38.
3. Richard Swenson, *Margin: Restoring Emotional, Physical, Financial, and Time Reserves to Overloaded Lives* (Colorado Springs: NavPress, 1992).
4. Charles Rassieur, *Stress Management for Ministers* (Philadelphia: The Westminster Press, 1982), 57.
5. James Glasse, *Putting It Together in the Parish* (Nashville: Abingon, 1979), 55–61.
6. Eugene Peterson, *Working the Angles* (Grand Rapids: Wm. B. Eerdmans Publishing Co., 1987), 77.
7. Walter Brueggemann, *Finally Comes the Poet* (Minneapolis: Augsburg, 1989), 82.
8. Ibid., 91.

H.B. London has served for a decade as director of pastoral ministries at Focus on the Family, Colorado Springs. He is known as a 'pastor to pastors'. Prior to his current assignment, he served congregations as a shepherd-leader for 31 years. He is author of *Refresh, Renew, Revive* and co-author (with Neil Wiseman) of *The Heart of a Great Pastor* and *They Call Me Pastor*. Dr London and his wife, Beverly, have two married sons and four grandchildren.

The Need to Flee – for Purity's Sake

H.B. LONDON

It is my privilege to interact with my colleagues who serve in pastoral ministry daily. Ministers – church leaders – are the group of men and women God has called to be caregivers of the souls of those in their flocks. This charge is a sacred and treasured calling. It is a hallowed entrustment from God and is worthy of deep soul investment to keep it pure and untarnished in the face of Satan's insidious attempts to defile every minister at numerous points on the journey.

At Focus on the Family we are interested in the soul health of our brothers and sisters in ministry. To that end we provide a free pastoral care line for ministers, Christian leaders and their spouses. About 60 per cent of the calls come from ministers; about 40 per cent come from their wives. Recently I asked the members of my staff who oversee this ministry what they have been hearing. Here is a sample:

A minister's accountability partner was struggling with issues in his life and could not continue the relationship.

One minister picked up a prostitute.

Another minister was dealing with members of his congregation who were wrestling with sexual issues.

Two pastoral colleagues were involved in affairs.

Another minister was struggling with homosexual feelings but had not acted out until he finally succumbed.

Still another was having romantic feelings for his administrative assistant.

One was emotionally attached to his secretary.

Three previous ministers had had affairs in the church. The current minister was dealing with the fallout.

A Christian leader had become addicted to pornography after being pure for 30 years.

A youth leader with a wife and three sons became emotionally involved with a woman in their church.

A professional counsellor called whose minister-husband had involved himself in multiple affairs.

A longtime minister had become hooked on Internet pornography.

One minister wanted to know how much he should tell his wife about the affair he had with the church secretary.

A senior church leader had just discovered that his associate used the leader's computer to go to pornographic sites.

A pastoral couple experienced an affair; they have left the ministry, but their teenage daughters are now struggling with their faith.

Every day as a 'pastor to pastors' I hear of colleagues who have given up because they succumbed to Satan's temptations.

A few years ago a colleague of mine confessed to his superior that he was involved in a sinful relationship. After serving more than 15 years in his assignment, he was immediately out of a job. His family separated; another family was torn apart. The media has profiled many stories like this in recent years – stories of persons in leadership and in public service who have chosen to break their trust of moral purity, tear families apart and bring shame to their names.

Why would men and women jeopardise everything so precious in life for a few moments of pleasure? They put at risk – and often give up – their families, their ministries and their reputations. Why? The answer, though not simple, is fairly easy to explain. When faced with temptation, when the warning deep in their minds and hearts screamed 'Run! Run! Run!' – they did not heed it and they failed to *flee!*

I offer a solemn caution for those who walk with God. The world sits outside our doors, and again and again Satan perches on our shoulders whispering enticing little temptations into our ears. But when he so subtly allures, the Holy Spirit is also present. Deep in the inner soul we recognise the authentic entreaty of the One who loves with the love of heaven. He urges, 'Run, run, as fast as you can! Move away! Don't stand there for even one moment!'

The Word speaks clearly and poignantly to this issue. Consider the message of the apostle Paul in Colossians 3:5–10:

Put to death, therefore, whatever belongs to your earthly nature: sexual immorality, impurity, lust, evil desires and greed, which is idolatry. Because of these, the wrath of God is coming. You used to walk in these ways, in the life you once lived. But now you must rid yourselves of all such things as these: anger, rage, malice, slander and filthy language from your lips. Do not lie to each other, since you have taken off your old self with its practices and have put on the new self, which is being renewed in knowledge and in the image of its Creator.

In verse 15 Paul says, 'Let the peace of Christ rule in your hearts.' There are several passages in the New Testament that urge the believer to 'flee'.

Flee Immorality

Paul clearly addresses the sacred relationship of the body to the Holy Spirit. 'Your body is a temple of the Holy Spirit' (1 Cor. 6:19). 'Flee,' he urges the Corinthian believers, everything that tempts to sexual immorality (v.18). Ephesian 5:3 says, '[Let there not] be even a hint of sexual immorality.'

The Old Testament gives us the story of Joseph and Potiphar's wife. Joseph literally ran – 'ran out of the house' (Gen. 39:12) – from the temptation and the potential of a broken life.

I share the messages and inquiries that came to the Focus on the Family clergy care line because they came from men and women called to pastoral ministry and Christian service. They are men and women not so unlike yourselves who have responded to the call, attended Bible college or seminary, studied the Holy Scriptures, and set out to minister the biblical message of grace and transformation. But somewhere on the journey Satan pursued them and began whispering enticements in their ears. He cornered them, and at some point they found themselves trapped.

Some found themselves in compromising counselling situations. Sometimes referred to as 'the syndrome of the soft shoulder', they began to communicate with a member of the opposite sex in a way they have not communicated with anyone for a long time. An emotional attraction developed and instead of fleeing, saying we must stop meeting, they rationalised, stepped across an invisible line, and then were trapped.

Some very innocently and unexpectedly saw a pornographic image on a computer. Rather than turning it off, they lingered. Soon they were trapped. One minister acknowledged, 'I viewed one image on my computer screen, and I have been captured ever since.' Why? Because that minister allowed his mind to centre on the wrong things.

The Way of Escape. 'Therefore honour God with your body' (1 Cor. 6:20). God's enabling grace is far greater than the enemy's temptations. Appeal to Christ's atoning sacrifice provides a way of escape for holding hallowed the most treasured of all relationships – with Him – as well as the priceless ones on this earth.

Flee Idols

In 1 Corinthians 10:11–14 the apostle Paul gives another warning. 'These things happened to them as examples and were written down as warnings for us, on whom the fulfilment of the ages has come. So, if you think you are standing firm, be careful that you don't fall! No temptation has seized you except what is common to man. And God is faithful; he will not let you be tempted beyond what you can bear. But when you are tempted, he will also provide a way out so you can stand up under it. Therefore, my dear friends, flee from idolatry.'

But what happens to us? Often we rationalise that we are strong enough to withstand the assaults on our faith. The attitude often is, 'I don't need to flee from that. I can change the rules. I'm strong enough. I've got what it takes to counter that temptation. I'll just adapt to my feelings. I will take control of things!' But the truth is we can't change the rules. We are not strong enough. We only kid ourselves when we rationalise that we are stronger than others. A part of God's plan to defeat temptation is to flee!

Why do I use the word 'flee'? It's a word that suggests that a person is in some kind of danger. It's a warning word, indicating there's something pursuing you that just might be stronger than you. This is not a scenario for standing and fighting. It is the time to get away from it. This is potentially an exploding bomb!

Many of you can quickly bring to mind at least three or four people in Christian service who in the last few years have moved away from a lifestyle of faith and into a lifestyle of rebellion. They fell prey to their former ways. Why? Because they thought the rules did not apply to them. They felt they were adequate or righteous enough to handle it. Sadly, they failed.

In my work at Focus on the Family I often experience this scenario. A minister calls and says, 'H.B., I'm going through some really tough times.'

I ask, 'Who are you accountable to?'

Often the minister responds, 'Well, not really anybody; I just don't trust anybody.'

'How is your relationship with God – your intimacy with Him?'

'Honestly, it's not very good.'

I say, 'Where's your strength coming from?'

He responds, 'Oh, I can handle this.'

You can't handle it! That's why Paul said, 'Flee from idolatry.' Don't stand there. Don't let it destroy you. Flee it!

The Way of Escape. 'He will also provide a way out so that you can stand up under it' (1 Cor. 10:13).

Flee Materialism

In 1 Timothy 6, Paul addressed the issue of materialism. He spoke of the 'root of all kinds of evil' being 'the love of money' (v.10). He then said, 'Flee from all this' (v.11).

What does an unhealthy attitude towards money do? What does materialism do? It causes a person to depend on his or her own resources and appetites instead of God's.

Arrogance can sneak into our lives and cause us to see ourselves as better or more significant than someone else because of what we possess or control. Paul says to his young son in the faith, 'Flee these things.' Materialism wields a destroying influence. The temptation can be very real. When the lottery frenzy is in full swing, it is so easy for a person to consider just for a brief moment, 'What would it be like to win? Wouldn't it be something just to have a few million pounds lying around?' We smile.

Many well-meaning, Bible-believing people have justified purchasing a lottery ticket from time to time by saying, 'Well, if I win, I'll be able to give a lot of money to the church. I'll be able to help my people.' A person can easily rationalise, 'I deserve several million pounds. I've lived a good life. Now I can have a lot of extra time to work for the Lord.' We smile.

Flee those kind of thoughts. Why? Because deep in our hearts we know that when we begin to think of riches, Satan will wave pound signs and power signs in front of us that will be spiritually destructive. Prosperity can easily destroy our motivation, our priorities and the person God intended us to be. Flee those things! All of us have known colleagues who spent far more time building earthly treasures than they spent investing in souls.

Fleeing is not just about resisting sexual temptation. It is about turning from those things that pollute our minds and tarnish the purity of our souls. The passion for 'things' tends to relegate God to a lower status, and ministry to business rather than a call.

The Way of Escape. 'Pursue righteousness, godliness, faith, love, endurance and gentleness' (1 Tim. 6:11).

Flee Evil Desires

I call your attention to one more 'flee' passage. Paul admonishes in 2 Timothy 2:22 to 'flee the evil desires of youth'. The apostle goes on to renounce the evils of bitterness, rage, anger, fault finding, jealousy and those things that dominate a person's heart and destroy the fibre of his or her spiritual life. An individual can suddenly be in a place that is morally compromising until at some point he or she becomes unable to break free from the trap.

Charles Wesley's hymn lyrics provide a tremendous aspiration:

I want a principle within
  Of watchful, godly fear,
A sensibility of sin,
  A pain to feel it near.
I want the first approach to feel
  Of pride or wrong desire,
To catch the wand'ring of my will,
  And quench the kindling fire.
That I from Thee no more may part,
  No more Thy goodness grieve,
The filial awe, the fleshly heart,
  The tender conscience, give.
Quick as the apple of an eye,
  O God, my conscience make;
Awake my soul when sin is nigh
  And keep it still awake.
If to the right or left I stray,
  That moment, Lord, reprove;
And let my spirit weep and pray
  For having grieved Thy love.
O may the least omission pain
  My well-instructed soul!
And drive me to the blood again,
  Which makes the wounded whole.[1]

The Way of Escape. 'Pursue righteousness, faith, love, and peace, along with those who call on the Lord out of a pure heart' (2 Tim. 2:22).

The Answer

The book of James provides an answer with specific directions for living the pure life. 'Submit yourselves, then, to God. Resist the devil, and he will flee from you. Come near to God and he will come near to you' (4:7–8). That's the answer. Intimacy with God! Submit and give yourselves a stronger defence.

I write from my heart. That is the reason I address you as though I had the privilege to talk with you in person. To each pastor or minister, Christian counsellor, teacher, professor, layperson, as well as to each one who has authority, influence and power – I beg you – be sure every area of your life is surrendered to God! 'Resist the devil.' Build a hedge of protection around yourself by loving God with all your heart, and by caring for your family. Make yourself accountable to someone. Put restraints on your life so that Satan cannot invade you. I challenge you to 'come near to God and he will come near to you'. That is a promise!

You may have felt the pain of watching persons you love destroy their lives because they didn't resolve to run from what was chasing them. I am sure you found it to be an exceedingly painful experience. We must not allow ourselves the same outcome.

The potential of falling to the wiles of Satan is real. You may be struggling with pornography. You may be toying with inappropriate emotional attachments to others. You may have sacrificed your intimacy with God because you have become so busy doing Christian things. You may be so wrapped up in your own profession that you are missing God's best plan. You have set your own course; you are playing by your own rules. 'Come near to God and he will come near to you.' That is a promise!

One day a friend said to me, 'H.B., what's chasing you?'

I said, 'What do you mean, "What's chasing me?" '

He said, 'What are those things in your life that you need to run from, to flee?'

That question prompted this chapter! A question like this might appear naive or elementary, but let me ask it anyway. What is chasing you? What in your life do you need to turn away from? Paul gives us at least four categories. Sexual temptation – flee from it. Idols – those things that become substitutes for God – flee from them. Materialism – allowing the things of this world to be more important than the things of God – flee from it. Evil desires – flee them.

Some time ago I read a devotional by Charles Swindoll entitled 'Lust'. He wrote, 'I think of the gentleman I met several years ago – a fine itinerant Bible teacher. He said he had been keeping a confidential list of men who were once outstanding expositors of the Scripture, capable and respected men of God ... who have shipwrecked their faith on the shoals of moral defilement. During the previous week, he said, he had entered the name of *number forty-two* in his book.'

Dr Swindoll said a chill ran down his spine when he heard the story. He wrote further:

> Lust is no respecter of persons ... Its alluring voice can infiltrate the most intelligent mind and cause its victim to believe its lies and respond to its appeal. And beware – it never gives up ... it never runs out of ideas. Bolt your front door and it'll rattle at the bedroom window, crawl into the living room through the TV screen, or wink at you out of a

magazine in the den ...

Lust is persistent. If it's knocked on your door once, it'll knock again. And again. You are safe just so long as you draw upon your Savior's strength. Try to handle it yourself and you'll lose – every time. This is why we are warned again and again in the New Testament to *flee* sexual temptations. Remember, lust is committed to wage *war* against your soul – in a life-and-death struggle – in hand-to-hand combat. Don't stand before this mortal enemy and argue or fight in your own strength – run for cover ... If you get yourself into a situation that leaves you defenseless and weak, if your door is left even slightly ajar, you may be sure that this ancient enemy will kick it open with six guns blazing. So don't leave it open. Don't give lust a foothold – or even a toehold.[2]

How very true! One minister said to me, 'I'm so tired of hearing people stand up in a conference and talk about Christian leaders and their moral failures. When can we get on to something else?'

I understood his desire. I wish it could be so. Unfortunately, Satan is real, and he's out to destroy the Church and to undermine families. Someone must continue to sound the alarm. This means we must exercise continual vigilance, focus on this terrific battle and appeal to the atoning work of Christ for victory. When the enemy knocks on the door and the door is not quickly slammed, all of a sudden he has a toehold. Without great care it is possible to find yourself hooked for all time.

When my aforementioned colleague announced that he had fallen morally, I was devastated. I was angry. I was hurt. In my weekly column, 'The Pastor's Weekly Briefing', I expressed my pain:

My reaction to these occurrences was at first anger, then disappointment, then compassion, and now self-examination. 'But for the grace of God, there go I' is a response that many have given. I am certain that a lot of you who read my words can think of those 'close calls', idle thoughts, and innocent acts that might have caused disaster in your ministry and family had it not been for the grace of God. We are all sinners saved by grace and all on various stages of the journey – but we are never safely home until we get home.

Dr Howard Hendricks, the noted professor emeritus at Dallas Theo- logical Seminary, once said, 'Satan will lie in the weeds for forty years if he needs to, to entrap one of God's servants. He is very patient. He will wait and he will watch for just the right moment – a moment that will do the greater damage to the Kingdom of God. He attacks and his successes are more frequent with each passing day.'

What are our lines of defence?

1. Intimacy with God
2. Right relationships
3. Adequate rest
4. Honest accountability
5. Meaningful ministry
6. Attitudes of joy and thanksgiving
7. A vigilant spirit

When our Saviour hung on the cross and shed His blood for all humankind, He had your name inscribed on His heart. He had called you, and He promised to protect you. When I ponder the sacrifice He paid for me and meditate on His unconditional love, I hear clearly the warning to flee the schemes of the enemy. I want to run as fast as I can – away from the evil one and back into His arms. I want to flee into the safety of His care! There is where my security lies – and so does yours.

Look around you. Where evil is pursuing you, so is the loving presence of our heavenly Father. He is in hot pursuit of His child. That's you, my friend. That's you!

Notes

1. Charles Wesley, 'I Want a Principle Within', in *Wesley Hymns*, comp. Ken Bible (Kansas City: Lillenas Publishing Co., 1982), no. 76.
2. Charles Swindoll, 'Lust', in *Killing Giants, Pulling Thorns* (Sisters, Oreg.: Multnomah Press, © 1978; © 1994 by Charles R. Swindoll, Inc.), 5–37. Used by permission of Zondervan Publishers.

For Further Reading

London, H. B., Jr., and Neil B. Wiseman, *Becoming Your Favorite Church*. Ventura, Calif.: Regal Books, 2002.

London, H. B., Jr., and Neil B. Wiseman, *They Call Me Pastor*. Ventura, Calif.: Regal Books, 2000.

London, H. B., Jr., and Neil B. Wiseman, *The Heart of a Great Pastor*. Ventura, Calif.: Regal Books, 1999.

London, H. B., Jr., and Neil B. Wiseman, *Married to a Pastor*. Ventura, Calif.: Regal Books, 1999.

London, H. B., Jr., and Stan Toler, *The Minister's Little Devotional Book*. Tulsa: Honor Books, 1997.

Larry Burkett is founder of Christian Financial Concepts, Inc. (now Crown Financial Ministries). Since 1976 he has dedicated his life and ministry to teaching biblical principles of financial management. He has published over 50 books with total sales of over two million. His daily radio broadcasts, *Money Matters* and *How to Manage Your Money*, are carried on over 1,100 outlets worldwide. Larry and Judy have four grown children and nine grandchildren. The Burketts live in Gainesville, Georgia.

5

Personal Financial Stewardship

LARRY BURKETT

In 1981 Mark Allen was called to serve as pastor of a new church. He and his wife, Belinda, bought an expensive house, and immediately they were strapped financially. They tithed but only because they knew that the church treasurer would know if they didn't.

Years later Mark reflected, 'I was upset with God. I thought that if we didn't have to tithe, we'd be OK financially. But our giving wasn't the real problem; not having a budget was. We had no idea where our money was going.'

Then Mark and Belinda read the book *Your Finances in Changing Times*, and they developed a budget. Soon their church gave them a generous increase in salary. They kept expenses at a minimum, and within three years their only debt was the mortgage on their house. In 1991 they paid off the mortgage.

The success the Allens experienced came from being good managers of God's provision. When He saw that they appropriately managed what they already had, God provided even more abundantly for them.

Could it be that's what Jesus meant when He said, 'Well done, good and faithful servant! You have been faithful with a few things; I will put you in charge of many things. Come and share your master's happiness!' (Matt. 25:21).

Ten years after paying off his mortgage, Mark Allen joyfully reports, 'We praise God that we're now able to give more to missionaries and other ministries than we were giving to creditors a few years ago. God really blesses when we do things His way.'

A minister holds a position of leadership as a representative of God to the flock. This position carries with it the vital challenge of an exemplary stewardship of time, talents and treasure.

The Spectre of Materialism

Our age is characterised by a consumer mentality. Priorities are often based on wants and desires instead of needs. Unfortunately, many Christians, including those in ministry, place their confidence in money and material things.

Our market-driven culture encourages building bigger barns in order to store more 'stuff'. This mind-set has already changed the hearts and lifestyles of too many Christians. God's people are entrusted with the privilege of setting an example of being the best possible managers of life and possessions.

Some people have an excessive desire to accumulate because of a fear of the future. They continually try to prepare for the unexpected. Jesus said, 'No-one can serve two masters. Either he will hate the one and love the other, or he will be devoted to the one and despise the other. You cannot serve both God and Money' (Matt. 6:24).

The point is not that it is wrong to be wealthy. There's no more sin in being wealthy than there is virtue in being poor. One cannot, however, be driven by wealth as a master and serve God.

The financial level at which God establishes an individual is up to Him. The willingness to serve Him at the financial level He provides is up to that person. A minister's attitude and level of contentment exhibited to those in his or her charge testifies to whether God or money is the motivating 'master'.

Consider the following suggestions:

Trust God as a conscious daily activity. Accept God's provision as His plan for your life. Find contentment in Jesus, the Source of the supply, rather than in the supply itself (see 1 Tim. 6:7–8).

Develop a long-range viewpoint. Serve God with patience. 'Therefore do not worry about tomorrow, for tomorrow will worry about itself. Each day has enough trouble of its own' (Matt. 6:34). As you interact with others, don't lose sight of God's longsuffering with you.

Pray diligently. Don't call attention to yourself (see Matt. 6:5–7), but don't let your prayer life be a secret to those you serve. '... pray continually; give thanks in all circumstances, for this is God's will for you in Christ Jesus' (1 Thess. 5:17–18).

Contentment

Money cannot buy contentment, but poverty certainly doesn't provide it either. Being contented doesn't necessarily mean satisfaction with circumstances; it does mean knowing God's plan for one's life.

Contentment is an attitude. When a Christian knows God's plan and believes God's peace is greater than the world's problems, he or she can be content.

Usually people are discontented not because they don't have enough; they're discontented because *others have more!*

If you desire to be content, note the following suggestions:

Establish a reasonable standard of living. When God provides a surplus, it doesn't mean it is to be used any way you want. It's important to develop a lifestyle based on conviction – not circumstances (see Luke 12:16–21).

Develop a giving habit. God expects us to help supply the needs of others. Don't worry about God or His people running out of money. 'At the present time your plenty will supply what they need, so that in turn their plenty will supply what you need. Then there will be equality, as it is written: "He who gathered much did not have too much, and he who gathered little did not have too little" ' (2 Cor. 8:14–15).

Determine appropriate priorities. Don't allow the urgent to take priority over the important. You and your spouse should establish mutually acceptable budgeting and spending priorities. It will help to make sure that you keep 'your lives free from the love of money and be content with what you have, because God has said, "Never will I leave you; never will I forsake you" ' (Heb. 13:5).

Acquire a gratitude attitude. Don't compare yourself with others. Be grateful. 'But if you harbour bitter envy and selfish ambition in your hearts, do not boast about it or deny the truth. Such "wisdom" does not come down from heaven but is earthly, unspiritual, of the devil' (James 3:14–15).

Refuse to have a fearful outlook. A hoarding attitude often comes from dwelling on the 'what ifs?' of the future. 'For God did not give us a spirit of timidity [fear], but a spirit of power, of love and of self-discipline' (2 Tim. 1:7).

A contented servant of Jesus Christ strives to have godly priorities, live a reasonable lifestyle and be a thankful giver.

Learn and Live God's Principles

Sometimes it's easier to commit money than it is to commit time and talent, but biblical stewardship involves managing all three.

The way a person uses money is the clearest outside indicator of his or her commitment to God. Jesus explained an essential spiritual truth by presenting it in a material way. 'For where your treasure is, there your heart will be also' (Matt. 6:21).

Stewardship of time is also a vital component of discipleship. It is a helpful time management exercise to list daily sleeping, eating and grooming time, subtract the total from the 24-hour allotment, then record for a week the total amount of time invested in kingdom endeavours. Priorities of time investment are revealing. The master a person chooses will be obvious. Jesus said, 'If anyone would come after me, he must deny himself and take up his cross daily and follow me' (Luke 9:23).

God is looking for leaders who'll put Him first in everything. 'Seek first his kingdom and his righteousness, and all these things will be given to you as well' (Matt. 6:33).

Throughout his military career, US Army Chaplain Major James Kannell and his wife, Elizabeth, have tried to share with others the biblical financial principles they've learned through a financial management course. And because she's a chaplain's wife, Elizabeth tells of her many opportunities to share with the wives of young soldiers.

Often invited to speak about financial issues on different occasions, Elizabeth says, 'I guess that word of my enthusiasm for biblical financial principles gets around. I simply share what we've learned and lived and then offer materials and information to young military families. The response has always been positive.'

Living out God's principles and sharing them with others brings joy and fulfilment.

Build a Budget and Live on It

Many congregations provide adequate compensation for their ministers, but others do not. A church's financial provision for its leader doesn't necessarily reflect its love for him or her. Small congregations often struggle to provide ministers with adequate incomes.

However, no matter what a person's income level – graciously adequate or barely making it – that person is responsible for handling God's provision as a faithful manager. That's why I'm so convinced that everyone, regardless of income level, should live on a budget.

A budget's purpose is to free a person, not confine. Proverbs 16:9 says, 'The mind of man plans his way, but the LORD directs his steps' (NASB). Living on a real budget illustrates that proverb.

There are very practical reasons for having a budget. A budget can free the planner from worrying about (1) making the annual insurance payment, (2) having money put aside for taxes or the mortgage, or (3) wondering whether enough money will be available for children's school supplies and clothes.

A budget is a plan that helps individuals or a family manage their money and live within their means. When a budget is developed with the goal of becoming free from the bondage of debt, a person quickly learns the benefits of following God's truth and receiving His promises.

Here's how a budget works:

- **The first part belongs to God.** 'Will a man rob God? Yet you rob me. But you ask, "How do we rob you?" In tithes and offerings' (Mal. 3:8). Christians are managers of what God owns and provides. God should get His part first.

- **The government takes its share.** Jesus said, 'Render to Caesar the things that are Caesar's; and to God the things that are God's' (Matt. 22:21, NASB). Taxes are a necessary component of providing a stable government for the security, corporate provision and peaceful living of all. What's left after tithes and taxes is called Net Spendable Income.

- **Family needs come next.** 'If anyone does not provide for his relatives, and especially for his immediate family, he has denied the faith and is worse than an unbeliever' (1 Tim. 5:8).

- **God says pay your debts.** 'The wicked borrow and do not repay, but the righteous give generously' (Psa. 37:21).

- **Faithful financial management results in a surplus of funds.** 'At the present time your plenty will supply what they need, so that in turn their plenty will supply what you need. Then there will be equality …' (2 Cor. 8:14). Management of finances with a budget maximises the benefits of any surplus. Wise use of God's provisions serves the best interests of a minister's family and establishes a good stewardship pattern for his or her congregation.

- **List monthly fixed expenditures.** Ongoing monthly expenses are then listed. These include tithe; taxes; household expenses; mortgage or rent; insurance; and so on.

- **Next, list variable expenses.** This category includes food, utilities, transportation, debt repayments, insurance, clothing, medical and dental, child care, and others.

- **Then, list all available income.** Salary, rents, interest and dividends, income tax refunds, and any other income sources.

- **This is for those on a nonfixed income.** If it's necessary to work part-time to supplement income, it might be helpful to use the method I recommend to those who work on commission or whose work is seasonal.

   For this type of budget a person first *conservatively* estimates the total annual income. Then *all* income is placed into a savings account and the *average* monthly income is drawn from that account each month. This allows surplus funds from higher income months to accumulate in the savings account to cover expenses during months of lower income.

The Scriptures offer this counsel, 'The prudent see danger and take refuge, but the simple keep going and suffer for it' (Prov. 27:12).

Budgets aren't all that mysterious, but they are necessary plans to help a person manage money and live within his or her means. Scriptural guidelines for budgeting are found throughout God's Word. For instance, Proverbs 27:23 says, 'Be sure you know the condition of your flocks, give careful attention to your herds.'

For those who don't have herds or flocks, God is probably saying, 'Be sure you know the condition of your food, housing, car and clothing budgets.' A budget is a good communication tool that allows a husband and wife to sit down together to discuss the amounts allotted and then come to a reasonable compromise.

Budgets are very simple: a specific amount of money is designated for spending, and a budget gives direction for spending it.

Some say, 'If the church keeps the minister poor, God will keep him humble.' Some seem to tout that as though it's in the Bible! Actually, God's plan according to the Scriptures is that a congregation should pay the pastor as a valued labourer. God can still keep him or her humble.

Nevertheless, even in a small church there are ways a congregation can legitimately relieve a minister of some tax burdens and at the same time help him or her financially.

If you have a church treasurer, or an accountant in your congregation, their expertise and advice could be invaluable.

Retirement

It is clear in the Scriptures that God's plan for delighting in Him and ministering in kingdom endeavours is lifelong. What we refer to as 'retirement' should simply be a transition to a different or less strenuous vocation – not a lapse into nonproductivity. Most people can't do at 65 what they did at 35 or 55, but they can do something.

For retirement planning I recommend vocational planning for the years beyond age 65 in addition to financial planning. In moving to an altered pace a minister may consider options such as speaking for pastors who need to be away from their pulpits. Or again he or she may consider writing, chairing the local ministers' fellowship, holding Bible studies in jails or nursing homes, getting involved in a local mission outreach, teaching a Bible class during the week or developing a hobby into a small business.

I encourage ministers not to quit. God has blessed them with too much ability and experience for them to just 'pack it in'. Life to the end is a stewardship issue – managing God's provision.

As regards financial planning for retirement, here are some things to consider.

The most disastrous financial circumstance for the majority of those who have retired is inflation. Inflation eats the heart out of many retirement plans at a time when most 'retirees' have little or no financial flexibility.

I suggest a three-pronged financial strategy to prepare for what we'll call retirement.

1. Although you may be living in church-provided housing, I believe the first phase of your long-term financial goal should be to own your home mortgage free. (Please understand that there are those with different views than mine on this subject.) Nevertheless, I believe owning a mortgage-free home is much better than trying to earn the income to pay rent or make mortgage payments during retirement. If you live in a church-owned house, try to buy a small rental property. Find some way to buy a house that could one day be your own – debt free.

2. After you've done your best to have a home with no mortgage, the second phase of your plan is to take some of the funds you were using for

mortgage payments and put them in a tax-sheltered plan to use for retirement. Be cautious at this point. If you're in a denominational church, your local tax office can help with this.

3. I suggest putting 10 per cent of your net spendable income in some long-range investments. Because you have a debt-free home, you could use some of the amount of your former mortgage payments. However, nothing escapes the manoeuvering of politicians. So I suggest you never put your total retirement savings in a tax-sheltered plan. These plans could become part of a government money pool from which others help themselves to the proceeds of your careful planning.

Too many are depending on the Social Security system for their retirement. Despite the current government 'fixes', the future of Social Security is not promising. Even so, as a 'sacred cow' it probably will continue to be used to the advantage of politicians.

Many ministers come to their 'retirement' years and have nowhere to live. They've always lived in church housing and have never invested in property they could rent out and later use as they grew older.

Often, the difficulties are compounded if there are no savings or investments because the minister has decided to 'live by faith'. There's certainly nothing wrong with living by faith (see Matt. 6:31–34), but there is something wrong with presuming on God because of not following biblical principles.

Those who don't plan during the higher-income *years of harvest* may find the senior *winter years* very lean. 'Go to the ant, you sluggard; consider its ways and be wise! It has no commander, no overseer or ruler, yet it stores its provisions in summer and gathers its food at harvest' (Prov. 6:6–8).

Even so, the same God who tells us to look to the ant for an example of planning for the future also tells us not to worry about tomorrow. The fear of doing without in the future causes many to rob God's work of the very funds He has provided.

In my opinion, God's Word encourages saving for retirement. Depending on your financial abilities and circumstances, those savings plans could be simple or complex.

No one has a more urgent responsibility or strategic opportunity to teach God's people His principles of stewardship and living than the minister. Through the grace of the Great Shepherd, the undershepherd can find delight in ministering biblical principles of stewardship. Many members of the flock will find fulfilment pursuing sound Christian principles with Christ as Lord.

THE LEADER'S EVERYDAY MINISTRY

William Willimon, STD, has been dean of the Chapel and professor of Christian ministry at Duke University in Durham, North Carolina, since 1984. He has served as pastor of churches in Georgia and South Carolina. In 1996, an international survey conducted by Baylor University named him one of the twelve most effective preachers in the English-speaking world. He is the author of 50 books. His articles have appeared in many publications including *The Christian Ministry, Worship,* and *Christianity Today.* His *Pulpit Resource* is used each week by over 8,000 pastors in the USA, Canada and Australia. He serves on the editorial boards of *The Christian Century, The Christian Ministry, Pulpit Digest, Preaching, The Wittenburg Door* and *Leadership.* He has given lectures and taught courses at many pastors' schools, colleges and universities in the United States, Canada, Europe and Asia. He is married to Patricia Parker. The Willimons have two children: William Parker and Harriet Patricia.

Call and Vision
Keeping the Big Picture

WILLIAM WILLIMON

To the murderer, Moses, hiding out in Midian, working for his father-in-law, God appears in a burning bush saying, 'I have heard the cry of my people. I am going to liberate them. And guess who is going to help me?' (author's paraphrase, see Exod. 3:7–10).

Moses protests. He is not good at public speaking (see 4:10). He has baggage. Yet Moses finds what succeeding generations found. Once the call to service comes, it is futile to wrestle with God. Once He has in mind that someone is a leader, one might as well relent with a deferential, 'Here I am, send me.'

Ministry is something that God does through the Church before it is anything we do. Our significance, as leaders, is responsive. We are here, in leadership of God's people, because we have responded to a summons, because we were sought, called, sent and commissioned by One greater than ourselves that our lives might be expended in work more significant than ourselves. Call begins it all.

What ministers do is a function of who ministers are. The great danger for clergy is not that we might 'burn out', to use a metaphor that is popular in our time, not that we might lose the energy required for ministry. Our danger is that we might 'black out', that is, lose consciousness of why we are here and who we are called to be for Christ and His Church. It is easy, amid the great demands of the pastoral ministry, to lose sight of that vision that once called us into being as pastors. Periodic refurbishment of our vision is needed. Take this book as an attempt to address the ethical crises of ministers by renourishing the vision by which they are called.

Vocation to service, in my experience, is one of the main sources of motivation for constancy in ministry. There are many times in the pastoral ministry when we see no visible results of our efforts, have no sense that people are getting better because of our work among them, have little proof of our effectiveness as priests. In those moments, our only hope is to cling to our vocation; to adhere to the sense that God has called us, rather than we ourselves; to know that God has a plan and purpose for how our meagre efforts fit into His larger scheme of things. God's vocation is the only ultimate validation of our ministry.

Years ago a friend of mine, Robert Wilson, distinguished sociologist of religion, conducted a survey among some clergy of the Episcopal Church and clergy of the Church of God, Anderson, Indiana, inquiring into their happiness and satisfaction with ministry. The Episcopal clergy had a much larger amount of financial compensation for their work; lived in larger, better-equipped parsonages; and had more generous pension schemes than the clergy in the Church of God. Yet the Episcopal priests were also far less happy and content in their ministry. Many of them showed low morale, deep unhappiness, particularly when compared to the Church of God ministers. Why?

Wilson said he thought part of the problem lay in the difference between how each group conceived their ministry. The Episcopalians, according to Wilson's interviews, saw themselves as 'professionals', well-educated, trained – though poorly employed and compensated – professionals. The Church of God clergy, on the other hand, saw themselves as called, willed by God to work in the Church of God, people sent on a mission.

'You can't pay people to do the things that ministers routinely must do,' said Wilson. 'They need to think God has called them, or ministry is miserable.'

Therefore the Church enjoins us to remember that we are called, that ministry is God's idea before it is ours, and that we are to seek God's help to be faithful to God's calling.

Colleague Stanley Hauerwas was recently asked about the moral confusion of contemporary clergy. Hauerwas said something to the effect that 'you have these people who get out of seminary thinking that their job is to "help people". That's where the adultery begins.'

What?

'So you have these clergy,' he continued, 'who have no better reason for being in ministry than to "meet peoples' needs". So little Johnny needs picking up after school. And Johnny's mother, since she is working, calls the pastor, who has nothing else better to do, and asks him to pick up little Johnny. And the pastor thinks, "Well, I'm here to help people." So he goes and picks up little Johnny. Before long the pastor meets a parishioner who is lonely and needs love, and then when caught in the act of adultery, his defense is that he's an extremely caring pastor.'[1]

I recalled what I thought to be, at the time, a rather silly article in *The Christian Century* by a pastoral care professor entitled 'Clergy Adultery as Role Confusion'. I wondered, what about 'Clergy Adultery as *Sin*'? But the more I have thought about it, the more I see that professor's point. In a culture of omnivorous need, all-consuming narcissism, clergy who have no more compelling motive for their ministry than 'meeting people's needs' are dangerous to themselves and to a church that lacks a clear sense of who it is.

Lacking a strong sense of their peculiar communal vocation, contemporary clergy have no means of resisting the tendency to wallow in the same psychotherapeutic mire as our people – meeting our needs; looking out for No 1; if it feels good, doing it; relentlessly scanning and feeding the ego.

We must be called – recalled – to the joy of being grasped by something greater than ourselves, namely our vocation to speak and to enact the Word of God among God's people. Sometimes ministers will say, 'I don't want to be treated as someone special, as a preacher. I just want to be respected as a person.' This point of view, so dear to modern, liberal notions of the self, is based upon the notion that we are most truly ourselves when we shed our socially imposed roles, when we attempt to forget we are spouses, parents and pastors so we can simply be 'one of the crowd' – just persons. Ministers are persons on whom hands have been laid. We ought not to seek to be free of such external, socially imposed attachments; in fact, such attachments make us more interesting persons than we would be if we had been simply left to our own devices. Morality is a matter, not of being unattached to any external determination, but of being free to think and act on the basis of our personal feelings of what's right. Contrary to the beliefs of liberalism, morality comes as a gracious by-product of being attached to something greater than ourselves, of being owned, claimed, commandeered for larger purposes, that is, *called*.

My own ministerial vocational ineptitude was vividly manifest to me a few years ago. Shortly after the war with Iraq in the 1990s, I received a note from one of the older members of my congregation, a note written on light blue stationery, neatly folded, a note written in a frail but still lovely hand.

'Have you preached on this particular episode? Have you mentioned it in one of your recent sermons? Now that I can't get out and about, I listen on the radio to your sermons, but I do not recall your having mentioned this.'

She was referring to a newspaper story (the clipping neatly folded within the same light blue envelope) about how American troops had buried alive as many as 600 Iraqi soldiers in their trenches during a battle.

'By the time we got there,' one soldier was quoted as saying, 'all that was left was hands and arms sticking up out of the sand.'

'What does this do to the moral character of our nation?' she asked, in graceful, antique handwriting on the blue notepaper. 'I grieve for the soul of our country. Where is the moral voice of our clergy in these matters?'

Her words stunned me into renewal of my vocation. The problem was not that I had been too timid in my preaching, too fixated in pop psychology to notice the ethical cataclysm taking place outside our sanctuary, too absorbed with the purely personal problems of my affluent congregation – although I was. My problem was not first a matter of morality. It was a problem of vocation, a need to be authorised by something more important than my own needs or even my assessment of the needs of my congregation.

I recalled a wonderful comment by Walter Brueggemann, something said to us preachers such as, 'If you are a coward by nature, don't worry. You don't have to be courageous to be a preacher. All you have to do is to get down behind the text. You can say, "This is not necessarily me saying this – but I do think the text says it." '

We can hunker down behind the text! Disjoined from service to the text, having no vocation to serve the Word, all I can do is to serve the congregational status quo, that is, run pastoral errands for the world as it is rather than let God use me to create a new world. This is the vision, the 'big picture', that is strong enough to sustain our ministry through the trials and tribulations of ministry. Anything else – a more modest sense of vocation such as 'helping people', 'just being there for people in need', or 'simply enabling the laity to do their ministry' – is too limp to sustain the pastoral ministry amid the rigorous demands of the gospel in collision with human sinfulness.

I urge all seminarians to read what is, in my opinion, one of the best novels of the late nineteenth century, certainly one of the best novels on the peculiar moral dilemmas of clergy. It is Harold Frederick's *The Damnation of Theron Ware* (1896). A young Methodist preacher is called to preach but called more so to advance socially through his preaching. Stifled by the confines of petty morality in the Midwestern town where he serves, the Reverend Ware longs for a larger stage on which to display his homiletical talents. His best friends – the urbane Father Forbes of the nearby Catholic church; Dr Ledsmar, the town's one social Darwinian; and Celia Madden, a wealthy connoisseur of the arts – represent all that Ware wants to be in life. The more these friends urge him to sample a social life out of his present reach, the less he regards his own ministerial vocation. His vocation becomes a career, a path up the social ladder through the flattering, eloquent art of his preaching.

Adultery is not far behind. When Ware finally confesses his love for Celia, she announces to him that his presumed 'improvement' has only served to render a once adequate pastor into a first-class bore. Ware eventually leaves the ministry, a victim of his own craving for status and recognition.

Ware's descent to the level of a rather common adulterer has nothing to do with his inability to meet his personal needs or with his being out of touch with his feelings as a man. His descent is related to his inability to be attached to his vocation as a preacher; it is related to the degeneration of his vocation into a mere means of occupational advancement. When that vocation becomes a mere means to an end, flaws in the preacher's character that may have been overcome by the preacher's attachment to his calling are magnified and the same banal temptations that afflict any other member of society are almost irresistible.

We must therefore develop those habits and practices that keep us tied to our vocation, that keep our originating vision before us.

1. We must find the opportunity periodically to refurbish our sense of being summoned, commissioned, called and ordained to be here in the pastoral ministry. Over the years I have learned that one reason why pastors return to seminary for a week of continuing education or to hear a series of lectures is that they are touching base with the origins of their ministry, recalling those early, formative days before their ministry became cluttered and distracted.

When I came to campus ministry, I found that I had to start each day with a time of Bible reading, guided reflection and prayer. I confess that I was rather haphazard about these devotional practices when I was in the parish. There I did not think I needed such discipline. But at the university, I found it essential to get focused at the beginning of the day, to tell myself, in effect, 'You are here as a priest, a prophet and a pastor, not simply as a second-level university administrator.' Looking back, I should have engaged in the same practice when I was a parish minister. It is so easy, amid the myriad of pastoral demands, to become distracted, to lose sight of that vision that put us here in the first place, to assume whatever culturally defined roles of success that society wants to place upon us, and thereby to lose the authorisation and validation of our ministry.

2. It is of the nature of the pastoral ministry to be susceptible to degeneration into triviality. Much that ministers do is small, mundane and not of large consequence, mainly because we are working on a human

scale, in one-to-one encounters with people, amid the daily routine of their lives. This is surely part of the power of the pastoral ministry, in being where people are, amid the daily and the mundane. However, this is also one of the temptations towards distraction in our ministry. Too many ministries degenerate into merely hospital visitation, mere church administration and mere preparation of a weekly public address. In my book (with Stanley Hauerwas), *Resident Aliens,*[2] we said there is a great deal of atheism in the practice of much contemporary ministry. Ministers go about counselling, preaching, teaching and administering as if God did not really matter, as if our efforts are the only efforts. Behind every busy, overworked minister is more than a touch of the atheistic sentiment that if we do not save the world and the Church, God will not do it. The Sabbath is recognition that it is not all left up to us and that our ministry is responsive, a derivative of the ministry of Jesus Christ, not a substitute for His ministry.

I therefore love that passage in Luke 10 where after having been sent out by Jesus to teach, preach and heal (in short, to do the same things Jesus does), the 70 return 'with joy', telling Jesus 'even the demons' submit to their teaching, preaching, and healing (v.17).

As they are reporting the results of their ministry, Jesus breaks in with, 'I watched Satan fall from heaven like a flash of lightening. See, I have given you authority to tread on snakes and scorpions, and over all the power of the enemy; and nothing will hurt you' (vv.18–19, NRSV).

What? The 70 are giving Jesus a rather mundane account of all that they were doing – healing, teaching, preaching – and Jesus breaks in with a vision of heaven, an apocalyptic vision in which our mundane, earthly work has heavenly, cosmic consequences. In our ordinary, daily round of ministerial activity, large matters are being worked out, Satan is being defeated, God is gaining His rightful kingdom, and our names 'are written in heaven' (v.20). The way to keep going in ministry is to keep that large vision before us.

3. One of the principal ways to keep the vision of our vocation, to keep clarity about our call, is through the weekly task of preaching. Week in, week out, to keep having to deal with Scripture and to allow Scripture to deal with us is one of the major sources of pastoral renewal. The Bible is so interesting, odd, life giving and soul forming. In that weekly rhythm of having to come up with something to say about Scripture, we are being formed and reformed in our vocation.

Too much of contemporary ministry is too human centred, engulfed by a sea of rather trivial human concerns. It is too easy to become sunk in the mire of people's problems, problems that have little to do with the demands of their discipleship and much to do with the trials and tribulations of being finite creatures. As a rule, Scripture always and everywhere is primarily about God and only secondarily and derivatively, about us. Scripture therefore keeps calling us back to the large questions, the great issues and the divine vision. We realise that the Church is called for more than to be another community service agency and that we, as leaders of the Church, are called for more than mere management of a volunteer organisation. Nothing less than life-and-death, large, kingdom issues are being worked out among us. Ministers are called for more than mere keeping house, soothing ruffled feathers and oiling denominational machinery. We are called to be active participants in the Jesus revolution called the gospel. Weekly, almost daily encounters with the Living Word keep that vision before us.

As we go about our work, we must look for opportunities to reiterate our vocation, the oddness of people like us being called for a spectacular adventure like this. I therefore enjoy, from time to time, reading again the words of the charge that the bishop gave me on the night I was ordained. I commend it to you as a way of revisioning the divine origins of our ministry, the seeping vision that is God's way in the world:

> *My sisters and brothers,*
>   All Christians are called through baptism
>   to share in Christ's ministry of love and service.
> This ministry is empowered by God's Holy Spirit
>   for the redemption of the human family and the whole of creation.
>
> You have been called,
>   by the spirit of God working in you,
>   to a representative ministry within the people of God.
> Christ's Body, the Church,
>   now confirms your calling through consecration or ordination.
>
> You are to lead the people of God in worship and prayer,
>   and to nurture, teach, and encourage them
>   from the riches of God's grace.
> You are to exemplify Christ's servanthood;
>   to build up the people of God
>   in their obedience to Christ's mission in the world;
>   and to seek justice, peace, and salvation for all people.

As representative ministers in the Church,
    you are to be coworkers with the bishops,
    deacons, diaconal ministers, and elders.
It is your task to proclaim by word and deed the gospel of Jesus Christ,
    to lead persons to faith in Jesus Christ,
    and to confirm your life in accordance with the gospel.

Remember that you are called
    to serve rather than to be served,
    to proclaim the faith of the Church and no other,
    to look after the concerns of Christ above all.

So that we may know that you believe yourselves
    to be called by God
    and that you profess the Christian faith,
We ask you:

Do you trust that you are called by God
    to the life and work of representative ministry in the Church?

I do so trust.

Do you believe in the Triune God,
    and confess Jesus Christ as your Lord and Savior?

I do so believe and confess.

Are you persuaded
    that the scriptures of the Old and New Testaments
    contain all things necessary for salvation
    through faith in Jesus Christ
    and are the unique and authoritative standard
    for the Church's faith and life?

I am so persuaded, by God's grace.

Will you be faithful in prayer,
    in the reading and study of the Holy Scriptures,
    and with the help of the Holy Spirit
    continually rekindle the gift of God that is in you?

I will, God being my helper.[3]

Notes

1. Hauerwas and I have attempted to think through some of these issues in our article, 'Ministry as More than a Helping Profession', *The Christian Century*, 15 March 1989, 282–84.
2. Stanley Hauerwas and William H. Willimon, *Resident Aliens: Life in the Christian Colony* (Nashville: Abingdon Press, 1989).
3. *The United Methodist Book of Worship* (Nashville: Abingdon Press, 1992), 688–89.

Michael Slaughter is chief dreamer of Ginghamsburg Church in Tipp City, Ohio, and a catalyst for change in the worldwide Church. His dynamic teaching, heart for the lost and innovative approach to ministry has led Ginghamsburg Church to outgrow all paradigms for a church in a cornfield. Mike challenges seekers and believers alike to wrestle with God and God's vision for their lives.

Preaching in a Postmodern Culture

MICHAEL SLAUGHTER

We are living in a pivotal time in history. The closing decade of the twentieth century evidenced unparalleled change. A seismic shift has occurred in the collective worldview. Many in today's culture no longer perceive truth via the closed, mechanical and scientifically based method that characterised the modern period (1500s–1960s). The postmodern worldview is dynamic, open and spiritual.

The discipline of preaching has remained unchanged essentially through the first 200 years of American history. Preaching biblical truth has been via cerebral, linear and rational methodologies corresponding to the methods of the age of the Enlightenment. Preaching was effective through this modern era because it adapted itself to the communication styles of the culture. Twenty-first-century communicators of this greatest story ever told will be effective because they understand the time and culture of the postmodern world.

Spirituality Is In

Postmodern people sense that the core of life and existence is spiritual. Peter Senge, leading consultant on current of change in the business community, notes that the bestselling books of this culture are about the new economy or Buddhism. Bookstores don a proliferation of spirituality titles on the bestseller list.

Western culture is living on the edge of a spiritual awakening. Postmoderns are open to the supernatural. They believe in gods, but they are not sure which one. The harvest is ripe with seekers who are exploring the possibilities of spiritual meaning from communicators who understand how to connect biblical truth with their felt needs.

One of these pre-Christian seekers named Scott came to Ginghamsburg Church through the invitation of Christian friends. He wrote this:

It is not difficult to explain why I first attended a Ginghamsburg worship experience in September 1997. Close friends told us about a service they had been to. Their description – in very accurate detail – led us to expect a fresh, even entertaining experience in the church. Indeed, that is what we found – great and 'nonchurchy' music, novel ways of presenting a message – and far from least, a stimulating talk by the presenter. The difficult thing to explain is why, at age 51, a lifelong agnostic like me would continue attending every week – absent only when circumstances absolutely prevented me being there, and why I really want to attend. I don't have an easy, short answer to that question. I found the pastor credible from the start. That was important to me. 'Credible' means you can believe in someone or something. They're authentic. If a credible person has faith, that implies to me that I might find their faith credible also.

Credibility and authenticity are traits of the Spirit that validate true spirituality. The actions of believers demonstrate the reality of the kingdom of God. Jesus said that by the fruit of an individual's life he or she would be known.

Modern preaching (18th–20th centuries) focused more on *proclamation*. Twenty-first-century communicators of biblical faith will include the *demonstration* of contagious faith in authentic community expressed through compassionate service. The postmodern preacher is more vulnerable and self-revealing than the preacher of the modern period. Today's preacher is more open to discussing the mysteries of faith.

Experience Is In; Explanation Is Out

We live in an experience economy. Restaurants, such as the Hard Rock Café, are built around themes and multiple-hour experiences. Many people spend money without even eating a meal.

Notice the phenomenon going on in bookstores today, particularly in America. Bookstores are becoming the new hangout! The brew is hot all day, and patrons partake as they browse. Shoppers are doing more than purchasing books. They are sipping coffee, catching up with friends, relaxing, listening to CDs, reading without the expectation to buy (yes, they are encouraged to try out the merchandise) – and some buy an occasional book. Today's bookstores provide an environment freighted with experiences. They are often equipped with comfortable, oversized chairs. Warm and inviting, the aura sends out a 'Come on in!'

Contrast these bookstores with libraries, at least as they were, often sterile environments, quiet and linear spaces where coffee and food were probably not allowed! The chairs were hard and straight. These rooms of stored information were not designed for experience. They were centres of information dissimulation – generally stiff, institutionally predictable, with limited visual or auditory sensory stimulation. Sound like any churches you are aware of?

Libraries and churches tended to be the structures of modernity. They targeted cerebral perception, while often neglecting the other senses. Bookstores engage all the senses.

Effective communicators of the twenty-first century understand that postmodern people are seeking an experience of God, not just a cerebral explanation. The first-century witnesses of this great truth were talking about an experience, an intimate encounter – not a cerebral belief system. 'That which was from the beginning, which we have heard, which we have seen with our eyes, which we have looked at and our hands have touched – this we proclaim concerning the Word of life' (1 John 1:1).

Postmoderns don't care about the Bible's infallibility as much as its integrity and moral value. They are not looking for theological comparisons but for spiritual connection and life relevance. The twenty-first-century communicator will act as a guide helping the postmodern seeker find the integrity of the eternal wisdom revealed in the biblical text without compromising biblical truth. The gospel is offensive, and many will walk away as they did from Jesus because they find its message unacceptable (see John 6:60).

Effective communicators of the gospel in today's culture understand the importance of the overall environment that engages all of the senses of the worship participant. From stained-glass windows to media screens, candles to stage lighting, pews to comfortable interactive seating, coffeepots to coffee shops, leaders in the new era are creating atmospheres of innovation. People learn best with all of the senses engaged.

Preachers who engage the twenty-first-century culture will affirm the mystery and paradox of the gospel. A paradox is two contradictory things existing together. A paradox means that sometimes truth is not 'either-or' but is 'both-and'. The Church was born in paradox. Jesus was both fully God and fully human. It is not rational! It doesn't make sense. We have often tried to communicate cerebrally – trying to prove the unexplainable. How do you explain or prove the Trinity? God is one yet exists in three Persons. Our brains try to push the facts one way or the other, yet we are people of mystery, formed by a Creator of mystery, and serving the God of mystery. Postmodern preaching will celebrate mystery, while churches of modernity will keep trying to master explanation.

Modern preaching in the twentieth century at times became issue centred and formed content around either liberal or conservative ideology. Postmodern preaching will need to focus on the awe-inspiring work of Christ, the power of His atoning sacrifice. 'When I came to you, brothers and sisters, I did not come proclaiming the mystery of God to you in lofty words or wisdom. For I decided to know nothing among you except Jesus Christ, and him crucified' (1 Cor. 2:1–2, NRSV).

The postmodern church is truly an ancient/future experience: stained glass and media screens, candles and stage lights, secular and sacred, young and old, believers and seekers together seeking an experience of God.

Asking the Right Questions

Jesus asked questions, 'Who do you say I am?' The disciples, at times wanting quick, easy answers, were frustrated at some of Christ's responses. 'But that's not what we asked you Jesus! You answered a question with another question. For heaven's sake, Jesus, we've got our pens out and our notebooks open. Now cut to the chase and tell us the answer – it would be so much easier!'

Jesus understood that true life-transformation is more about asking the right questions rather than about always giving the correct answers. Real growth happens as we struggle with significant questions. If we are not struggling, we are snoozing. Often we have offered explanations in our churches, and people have accepted them and dozed on because the Church is not dealing with the hard questions. 'Who do you say that I am?'

We must become as little children. The average child asks an average of 106 questions a day, yet by the time we become adults, the average is reduced to a mere six! We have forgotten how to be curious. For many, the church is not a safe space to ask honest life questions for fear of harsh judgment and criticism. Preachers in this new era must make room for tough questions and trust the Spirit to change people's lives.

My friend Scott was given the safe space at Ginghamsburg Church to ask honest questions and to give what some considered wrong answers. The Spirit can do amazing things in an environment of trust and love.

I guess I'm what you consider a seeker. I started out two years ago as an agnostic. Since then, through a convoluted path, I've come to consider myself tentatively 'Christian.' All along I've tried to translate things Christian people say into meanings that I can embrace. It seems to work for me. I translate and accept them, and sometimes later I find that I don't need to translate them anymore. When I think of a church setting out to make an appeal to a seeker like me, it's a big challenge to take on. Similar maybe to knowingly adopting children who have highly limiting and incurable challenges – physical or mental. The kind of challenges only a miracle can overcome. For us, actions completely drown out words. True Christian behavior is the only thing that can win me. I'm learning there's nothing more persuasive or powerful than that in the human range of acts.

Seekers are not *i* dotters or *t* crossers and are least likely to be reached by folks who are. Give us leaders who know that God is much too great to be threatened by wild questions or unconventional speculation. Fear not!

Evidence and argument didn't make God ultimately real for me. I don't know what did. Maybe it was just the concentrated and extended focus – listening for God. If I am a seeker, what am I still seeking? ... I want an encounter with a real God. I want there to be someone who can take me higher, and I have begun to have that. One day, and it was just a day nothing much happened, I suddenly knew there was God and that God was present around me.

Scott Parsons

Postmodern preaching begins with the relaxed atmosphere that greets people at the door. Warm expressions of welcome, information adequately provided, and the aroma of coffee beckon guests to 'come on in' and experience. Once inside the worship area, the atmosphere is thematically provided to prepare hearts for the experience ahead. Candles are lit. Instrumental music is playing – jazz or Celtic. The media screen wallpaper depicts a selected weekend metaphor, a twenty-first-century stained-glass window. Soft lighting and a visual stage display draw the eyes and begin connecting hearts before the Word is spoken. It is a multisensory church – a safe space for hungry hearts, a place to call home, an experience of community. In this atmosphere of authentic biblical community, people faithfully demonstrate the love and presence of Jesus and the preaching event is experienced.

Electronic Media – The Language of the Culture

How do you design a worship experience in a post-literate age where most people receive their information from a source other than the printed text? We turn back to the future and ask, 'How did the Church do worship in a preliterate culture?'

The premodern church made rich use of visual imagery. The mediaeval churches in Europe depended on the visual arts to tell the biblical story. These included elaborate wood and stone carvings, massive stained-glass windows, tapestries, frescoes and detailed paintings by the masters. Dramas were used as interludes in the sermons. This appeal to the senses made the church the best multimedia experience in town. Candles and incense added to the multisensory environment.

We live in an age where text, audio and video converge into the new mixed genre that is labelled multimedia. This convergence drives us back to the future to design worship experiences that are tactile and multisensory. Traditional, abstract liturgy no longer speaks the language of a postmodern culture. Our worship-preaching forms must bridge a person's mind with their feelings, emotions and cultural connections. Premodern worship centres evoked awe and wonderment. Electronic media is no longer an option for the church. Electronic media is the language of our culture.

Churches all over the world have already embraced this technology into their worship experience. Our worship attendance grew from 1,200 to over 3,100 in the first 2½ years after incorporating media into our weekly worship celebrations.

We use electronic media in an interactive form with music, literature, art, drama, writing, poetry and movie clips. We borrow ideas from David Letterman's 'Almost Live' spots, in which he appears to leave the studio by playing clips that have been produced earlier. With this technology, I am able to go 'on location' in the middle of my sermon. Electronic media opens the door to unlimited creative possibilities.

Postmodern preaching does not stand by itself. It is intricately interwoven into a multisensory, interactive, innovative worship experience. The postmodern preacher is, first and foremost, a spiritual leader who is authentic, vulnerable and accountable. He or she does not create the sermon in isolation but works with an innovative team. They are moved forward by the breath of the Spirit – and are undisturbed by change.

For Further Reading

Hanson, Handt, *Mission-Driven Worship: Helping Your Changing Church Celebrate God*. Loveland, Colo.: Group Publishing, 2001.

Morganthaler, Sally, *Worship Evangelism*. Grand Rapids: Zondervan Publishing Company, 1999.

Slaughter, Michael, *UnLearning Church: Just When You Thought You Had Leadership All Figured Out*. Loveland, Colo.: Group Publishing, 2002.
Out on the Edge: A Wake-up Call for Church Leaders on the Edge of Media Reformation. Nashville: Abingdon Press, 1998.

Sweet, Leonard, *AquaChurch*. Loveland, Colo.: Group Publishing, 1999.
SoulTsunami: Sink or Swim in New Millennium Culture. Grand Rapids: Zondervan Publishing House, 1999.

Jesse Middendorf, DMin, is a general superintendent in the Church of the Nazarene. He has served as pastor of several growing churches, including 10 years as pastor of Kansas City First Church of the Nazarene. From 1985 to 1991 he was superintendent of the Northwest Oklahoma District Church of the Nazarene. He has written numerous articles for religious periodicals, authored chapters in several books, and is the author/editor of *The Church Rituals Handbook*. He and his wife, Susan, have three children: Jon, Marlo and Jim.

Pastoral Leadership and Administration

JESSE MIDDENDORF

Few experiences are more thrilling to me than flying a single-engine light aeroplane. Managing the variety of responsibilities requires that the pilot be attentive to the engine, the instruments, the 'attitude' of the craft, the weather and numerous other issues. A careful process of balancing the many forces at work keeps the aeroplane in the air. While balancing many responsibilities, the pilot must maintain an intense focus while not being consumed by any one of them.

An aircraft in flight is itself the object of a series of delicate balances. The forces of lift and gravity, thrust and drag – all are at work, helping the plane maintain a safe speed, hold its altitude, proceed along a planned route and arrive at a desired location.

The pilot learns very quickly that an aeroplane is designed to fly. It does not require the pilot to do the 'flying', but that the pilot direct and manage the aeroplane so that it may safely do what it was designed to do.

Aeroplanes are awkward on the ground, but once airborne, they provide rapid transportation towards a specified destination or great enjoyment for those who love soaring through the air.

The design of an aircraft is also a delicate balance of characteristics that enable it to function in two very distinct environments. On the ground, the wings are a liability. They protrude from the sides of the fuselage at a distance that makes them awkward in the cramped spaces around the hangar or in parking areas. The wheels are a necessity, providing capability for steering around the obstacles that might impede its progress towards the runway. Once a skilled pilot is at the controls, the awkward wings become an asset. On the runway, at the proper speed, the wings provide the lift necessary for the plane to leave the ground environment and soar into the sky. But once in the air, the wheels, so necessary for the ground environment, become a liability, creating drag, slowing the aircraft they so effectively supported while on the ground.

The arena of flight is a proper analogy for the task of leadership in the Church. The task of leadership requires a careful balance of the many aspects to which a pastor/leader must give attention.

Leadership – a Vital Necessity

Leadership is not optional to the pastoral office. Administration and organisation are values necessary for the proper functioning of every ministry. Leadership is at the heart of a balanced ministry.

And yet God, in His infinite wisdom, has not found it necessary to call into ministry only those persons who are gifted in leadership and administration. On the contrary, the varieties of gifts and abilities found in the pastoral corps and among the lay leadership of the Church, reveal a shocking diversity. Men and women of every conceivable strength and capability are found giving effective leadership in churches and ministries around the globe. This magnificent mosaic is a testimony to the creative breadth of the Holy Spirit's work in the Church of Jesus Christ.

But the diversity of gifts does not lessen the necessity for leadership in the Church. Whatever the gifts, interests or abilities of the minister, leadership and administration are vital components of the work of every ministry.

The development and application of leadership and administrative skills is necessary for every minister. While for some the development comes easily, perhaps even intuitively, the necessity of further developing and honing leadership gifts is no less important.

For the majority of people engaged in ministry, learning principles of leadership and administration requires disciplined effort, sustained application and careful study. It may not come easily and may indeed be difficult and forbidding. But leadership must occur. Leaders must learn to lead.

Every church deserves competent leadership. Every minister is responsible for providing adequate, balanced and effective leadership in his or her ministry. The claim of a minister that he or she is not 'gifted' in leadership does not release him or her from the leadership necessity.

But how do we get there from here? What does the leadership task require? How do we become effective leaders?

First, let's provide some basic definitions for our discussion. For the purposes of this chapter, leadership is defined as the ability to influence others towards a desired future. It is the willingness and the ability to carefully steward the resources of the Church towards the fulfilment of its mission. It is the stewardship of the people, the values and the legacy of the

Church, and its focus is found in relationships.

People are the heart and the spirit of the leadership endeavour. Conceptions of power and privilege are out of place in church leadership, antithetical to its purposes, and destructive of the ethos out of which the Church derives its identity as the Body of Christ, the community of faith, the servant-people of God.

Church administration is a leadership function and consists of the organisation of the people and the resources of the Church for the accomplishment of the objectives of the kingdom of God. It cannot be done unilaterally. It is, by the very nature of the task, highly relational in its pursuit. But it is of necessity very focused. Administration presses towards the objectives with clarity and intentionality. It refuses to be distracted from the goal but proceeds with grace and dignity.

Some have said that the first responsibility of leadership is to define reality, and the last is to say 'thank you'. Definitions of leadership that are categorical and fixed are hard to pin down. This task consists, however, in discovering, unleashing and polishing the variety of gifts that people bring to an organisation so that they may work together in a harmonious whole to 'get the job done'.

Striking the Balance

Like flying, leadership is a balancing act. It requires careful attention to the delicate balance that must often be struck between the variety of pressures that are at work in the leadership environment.

One of the dimensions of leadership that demands the most of the effective leader is managing change. The very purpose of leadership is to effect change, to provide the motivation for and direct the energies of others towards the fulfilment of the objectives of the church or ministry. The wise leader will always be attentive to the threats inherent in facilitating change in a local church. He or she must develop a high degree of tolerance for the processes necessary to effect change, stabilise the changes made and prepare the church for the next stage of change. It is a time-intensive endeavour. It requires persistent attention on the part of the leader and his or her team of workers so that the trajectory of the church's activities and relationships contribute toward the fulfilment of the goals of the church.

In order for a minister to be an effective leader, to navigate the environments through which leadership must move, a delicate balance must be struck between several pairs of competing poles. These poles describe the arena and the potential obstacles through which every effective leader will move.

The first balance the leader must strike is between passion and patience. Passion is better described than defined. It is seen in the pages of Scripture in the likes of Nehemiah and Ezra. These two Jewish exiles burned with a passion to return to Jerusalem. They were driven to rebuild the broken walls, to restore the ruined city, to reconstruct the Temple and to reinstate the worship of Yahweh.

The passionate letters of Paul to young Timothy and to the churches at Philippi and Ephesus demonstrate an inner drive, a fire, a *passion*. This energy of soul characterised the entire ministry of the apostle. By his own testimony, Paul was willing to endure anything in order to make Christ known, to establish the Church, and to equip the leadership of congregations everywhere.

The passion of John and Charles Wesley refused to die when pulpits and lecterns were denied them in the established churches of eighteenth-century England. Instead they went to the fields and the mines, to the teeming masses in London's squalid slums, and preached the gospel. They established the Methodist classes, bands and societies so forcefully and effectively that they helped save England from the destructiveness of revolution that so convulsed France.

Passion is a necessary element in effective leadership. It is the inner drive that motivates a leader to expend himself, to deny herself, to focus on the goal, the objective, the mission, the vision. Without passion, a leader is insipid. Few will follow, and those who do are frustrated and ineffective.

Passion is not a personality trait. It is the deep fire within the leader that burns consistently. It may be found in the nonviolence of India's Gandhi, or in the fiery determination of GE's Jack Welch. It may be heard in the eloquence of Martin Luther King Jr. or in the quiet consistency of First Lady Laura Bush.

Passion is founded on a clear sense of purpose. It has about it a kind of transcendence. When combined with the conviction of a divine call, it provides the substantive basis on which spiritual leadership is developed.

It does not require the dynamism of eloquence or a charismatic personality, nor does it mean that passion naturally goes with a position or title. Passion is an intangible inner conviction that burns just beneath the surface. It enables a person to influence others whether or not titles or positions are granted.

In the Church, leadership without passion is mechanical and uninspiring. Pastors whose only claim to leadership is the position they hold, whose leadership is not infused with a single-mindedness towards the mission of that local church, will seldom have a positive impact on others. But consumed with passion for the mission, even an awkward personality can inspire others to be more focused on the fulfilment of the mission.

Passion for God, for the Church of Jesus Christ, for lost and broken people and for holy excellence are characteristics that burn in the heart of every effective pastor. Passion is the 'fire in the bones'.

But passion must be balanced with patience in the effective leader. The zeal that burns within the heart and soul of a pastor must be deliberate. It requires that the leader be sensitive to the pace at which organisations can respond. A remarkable amount of patience must be exercised when the leader forges a team out of the disparities that always confront a leader.

Effective leadership requires that the passion be conveyed to those who follow. It requires that a leader recruit and coalesce a group of people into an effective and focused team, working together to accomplish their objectives. Leadership requires relationships. Relationships require work. And the work of relationship requires patience.

Leaders earn credibility over time, by willingly investing themselves in inculcating their vision and passion into the hearts and minds of others. The patience required is not easily managed in the passionate leader, one gripped by a sense of mission. All the inner resources are marshalled around fulfilment, accomplishment. Without cultivating patience, the leader becomes frustrated with the necessity of placing his or her timetable on the altar as he or she develops the credible relationships, the shared passion and the necessary resources for the task ahead.

The single-minded leader must pour himself or herself into the task of bringing others along. Effective leaders are not loners. The mission of the Church is not a solo accomplishment. The driven type A personality so often epitomised as the ideal leader can easily become a liability in any volunteer organisation but especially in the Church. Leadership requires patience with the processes of developing 'buy in' among the constituents.

The passionate, patient leader is not indolent or passive. This leader is proactive. This leader seeks out others. He or she intentionally moves towards potential conflict with grace and openness and does not force his or her will on others. Leadership requires passionate patience, and that patience must be expressed towards God, towards the Church of Jesus Christ, towards the lost and broken of the world, and towards the processes so necessary to holy excellence.

A second balance that must be struck is between creativity and faithfulness. Leadership and the administration of the Church also require great creativity. And yet what other organisation on earth is as likely to resist creativity and change than the Church? How easily the threat of change seems to dismantle relationships between pastor and people.

Yet again, creativity is one of the primary qualities of the effective leader. The ability to find innovative approaches to staid and routine ministries and programmes can bring new life to a congregation. But creativity finds its best energy in the context of faithfulness.

We were in a rut! The grand old church had a marvellous history, and its roots were deeply embedded in the soil of traditional ministry. But our neighbourhood was anything but traditional. The vast majority of the homes were less than 10 years old. Young families were moving into the area with unprecedented rapidity. Developers were building homes at an amazing, even alarming rate. Schools could not keep up with the pace of growth. Road-widening projects tied up traffic, and busy commuters passed us by with barely a glance.

In order to 'compete', to make ourselves more than a nondescript building on a busy corner, we had to think outside of our normal patterns. The challenge required a profound commitment to discovering and implementing creative approaches to reaching the community. Task forces were formed, populated with young members of the fellowship. They asked open-ended questions of their neighbours, seeking to know what it would take to reach the rapidly growing community with the message of the Church.

Before long the face of the church began to change. The visibility of the church increased through neighbourhood events planned for non-attenders. Service projects, friendship gifts and community involvement opened new doors for conversation with nearby residents. Before long, dozens of new families began to visit, some returning for special events, others identifying with the church as regular attenders.

In order to break through in the neighbourhood, we had to first break through in the church. The task of discovering new approaches to reach outsiders required hours of creative efforts to convince, recruit, train, and motivate a whole new cadre of workers *in* the church.

The leadership challenge was to assist a once flexible and creative old church to begin to think creatively again. This required that we examine our methods of communicating with the community. We had to be willing to risk embarrassment by asking questions of the very people we hoped to influence. We had to be open to their perceptions of the church, their fear of the church, and their suspicion of our motives in asking the questions. We had to be willing to challenge our own perceptions and expectations of how we were seen in the community. And we had to develop new methods of communication that were consistent with what we were learning about our community.

Creativity in method requires a massive effort at creativity in how planning and organisation are accomplished. Committees of long standing have to be honestly examined. What is their purpose? What is necessary according to legal and institutional requirements, and what is the product of unstated assumptions that have developed without conscious thought or strategic intent?

Creativity is by its very nature a threat to established organisations. In many cases, a variety of 'stakeholders' are engaged in assuring that what has been will be. They are often, quite unconsciously, deeply disturbed by any effort at creatively examining the methods and organisation of the church.

The wise leader will not be discouraged or surprised by the uneasiness that accompanies a careful study of the practices and methods of the church. He or she will understand that comfortable routines and methods grow out of experience that is not always subject to objective evaluation. Methods are often deeply embedded in the self-identity of a congregation, and opinions regarding their effectiveness will often take on spiritual dimensions. To examine or question the methods seems, to most church people, to call into question the very existence and stability of the church. In the conservative social structures of the church, what we do is who we are. How can you change that!

But careful leadership will recognise the opportunity to help the church examine its purposes, its objectives and its faithfulness to the Great Commission. The leader will not fear the task but will be carefully sensitive to the inner struggle that creativity will produce. He or she will not fear to help the church examine its methods but will see to it that in the examination, faithfulness to the character, values and beliefs of the Church are reaffirmed, solidified and celebrated.

The wise leader will realise that the creativity of the church cannot afford to destroy the character of the church. It is important that what people are invited to become a part of be unmistakably and unapologetically *the Church*.

The effective leader must utilise all the creative methodologies and approaches possible, consistent with the deeply held beliefs and values that brought the Church into existence. Creativity must be balanced with faithfulness.

Faithfulness must not be defined in terms of unwillingness to change methods and approaches. But creativity dare not disregard the core values and beliefs that give the Church its reason to exist. The Church is not just another institution or organisation. It is the Body of Christ. It is the fellowship of the 'called-out ones', the *ekklēsia*, the people of God. Its values and beliefs are not amorphous and fluid. They are based on the truths of Scripture, on the experiences of its founders and members, on the historical formulations of belief that have proved true through generations and centuries. And it is the product of the careful and deliberate thinking of its forebears. It is not subject to the kinds of 'creativity' that would undermine the doctrinal and ethical norms that brought it into existence.

And yet it is important to acknowledge how deeply embedded are our beliefs in the *way* we do things. The wise leader will not disregard the agony of church people who have a hard time believing that examining and reshaping the methods by which the Church communicates its message is not the same as challenging the beliefs and ethics of the Church. He or she, the leader, must not become angry or bitter towards those whose initial reaction to changing methods is horror and dismay. Striking this balance will require a deeper commitment to maintaining the relational integrity of the Church. It will mean longer periods of time spent in communicating, not just once or twice, but repeatedly, carefully, compassionately and passionately. It will require that the leader be committed to carefully leading people through the agony of change, without abandoning them, so that they may come to understand and embrace a change of methods as a natural expression of the Church doing its work of mission throughout history.

A balance must also be struck between vision and organisation. Here is where the critical interface between leadership and church administration finds expression. Vision is the ability to communicate a desired future. It is much more than the product of the inspiration given to any one individual, especially in a church. It is the product of the shared view of the leader and those who are the frontline workers and organisers who carry the vision forward.

The nature of the Church is expressed in community. It is not a one-man show (or a one-woman show, for that matter). It is the gathering up of the gifts, abilities and vision of the whole, inspired by the Holy Spirit and brought to focus and passion through the gifts and passion of a pastor/leader.

Visionary leadership is necessary in the Church, but it does not automatically reside in the person called 'pastor' in a given local church. It may well be that the role of the pastor is to help give expression to the corporate vision growing out of the passionate engagement of the people in the Word, with the community, and with the mission of a local church.

A body of people, providentially brought together in a given time or place, may well need the catalysing influence of a leader to be gripped by the possibilities that lie before them.

A minister who has carefully analysed the resources of the local church and the needs of the community in light of the Great Commission cannot help being gripped by possibility. The resources do not need to be extensive, and the community does not have to be large, but the fact that there are people who know Christ living near people who do not means that mission is not only possible but mandated.

A minister may too easily assume that the straight-line logic of the previous statement gives the right to berate a church for the 'failure' to fulfil the mission of the Church. But the reality, proved true throughout the history of the Church, is that the Church has always needed a visionary leader to bring focus, passion and sacrificial effort to bear. Every congregational situation is different. The personalities of ministers and lay leaders vary across all the possible measures and configurations. No church will respond to every pastor, and no pastor will be equally effective in every church. But no pastor can avoid the necessity of helping a local church craft a meaningful and definable vision for its work. Church effectiveness depends on a clear sense of what God has called the Church to do, on a clear sense of what part the local church plays in fulfilling the mission, and on the vision developed in that place for that church.

But vision alone is not sufficient. The vision must take wings, grip the hearts of people, and thrust them into the fulfilment of the vision. Vision rides on the wings of organisation.

Paul wrote to young Timothy, 'Those things you have heard from me, you are to teach to faithful people who will be responsible for teaching them to others' (2 Tim. 2:2, author's paraphrase). The necessity of organisation is inherent in the nature of the Church. Without careful, thoughtful and well-planned organisation, the Church may well spend much time, money and relational 'capital' and see little or no results. It requires the careful organisation of people who have been given purposeful assignments, with genuine responsibility, and who will agree to authentic accountability to get the job done.

Church leadership and administration are not optional components of the pastor's task. They are necessary to effective ministry. To claim a natural inability to 'lead' or 'administer' is to miss the point. A pastor may not be strong organisationally or administratively, but there are resources available to help pastors hone the skills and develop the principles of effective leadership. But the effort of leadership will never be reduced to zero. Leadership training and enrichment are not intended to eliminate the effort required for planning, leading and organising. Those resources and opportunities for learning are intended to reduce the amount of time necessary for 'redoing' or 'undoing' poorly conceived leadership strategies. No leader will ever do it perfectly. No plan of organisation will work everywhere. But the principles, the 'laws' of leadership, can make the effort more effective wherever the pastor finds himself or herself.

Pastors who seek to lead the church without giving extensive time to striking the delicate balances in leadership and administration will be flying with one wing clipped. It may well be the explanation for why so many seem to feel they are running in circles.

But the wise pastor who sees leadership and administration as the means by which the divine call is implemented in his or her ministry will find the church responding with deep appreciation, with willing sacrifice and with passionate commitment to fulfilling the vision God has given.

Here is my prayer for your ministry: May your love of God be reflected in your love of learning. May your love of learning enable effectiveness in leadership. May your effectiveness in leadership be seen in the lives of your people. And may the lives of your people, through the power of the Holy Spirit, change the world.

Ron Blake is director of Clergy Services in the Church of the Nazarene. Prior to assuming this post, he served 20 years as a pastor of growing churches. Ron and his wife, Susanne, have one son, Bennett, and enjoy keeping up with his high school activities. The Blakes live in Olathe, Kansas.

Pastoral/Congregational Care in the 21st Century

RON BLAKE

In the recent past, pastoral care was a major part of the minister's job description. The description included visiting the ill and bereaved within the established church community. Congregations valued this aspect of pastoral care. Through emerging leadership literature, other models of pastoral ministry are now put forward. The minister may be viewed as a CEO, a motivator or a vision caster who details the mission, gives direction to staff and keeps everyone focused and satisfied. For many, pastoral ministry has become more complex. One minister said, 'The rules have changed, and no one bothered to tell us about the changes.'

Pastoral care has always been considered a part of a minister's responsibilities. Pastoral search committees usually ask 'pastoral care' related questions during interviewing such as, 'Do you visit parishioners?' 'Do you make hospital calls?' and 'Do you make contact with visitors?' There is an unspoken, and sometimes not so unspoken, expectation that the minister will mingle with the people. He or she will be there when needed, available to offer consolation, comfort and advice, and will be 'on call' as a doctor is on call. Because of rapidly changing pastoral ministry models, the expectation and the reality have been on a collision course, and in some locales they have already collided. Before we consider further the changing paradigm of pastoral and congregational care, let us seek the counsel and wisdom of the Holy Scriptures.

The Bible contains poignant truths and insights regarding pastoral care. In Acts 6 we are told that the Grecian widows were being overlooked in favour of the Jewish widows. Whether this was a perceived slight or a real offence is not entirely known. Either way, the disciples discerned that the problem needed to be resolved. They did not view ministry and serving through Western 21st-century lenses but through Jesus' explanation of servanthood. It was, after all, Jesus who said, 'Whoever wants to become great among you must be your servant' (Matt. 20:26). On Jesus' last night of earthly ministry He washed the disciples' feet. He modelled servant leadership long before books were written on the subject.

Acts 6:3 gives the standard for those who were selected to wait on tables. It says, 'Brothers, choose seven men from among you who are known to be full of the Spirit and wisdom. We will turn this responsibility over to them ...' The biblical qualifications for those serving in this Early Church ministry were (1) Spirit-fullness and (2) wisdom. These qualities are vital for pastoral ministry candidates today. Leaders who minister 'care of the soul' must be filled with the Holy Spirit. Likewise, serving people requires wisdom.

Another passage provides instruction on this subject:

> Be shepherds of God's flock that is under your care, serving as overseers – not because you must, but because you are willing, as God wants you to be; not greedy for money, but eager to serve; not lording it over those entrusted to you, but being examples to the flock. And when the Chief Shepherd appears, you will receive the crown of glory that will never fade away. (1 Pet. 5:2–4)

Peter makes it clear that as leaders we are to be shepherds to the flock under our care. Ministers do not serve just because they have to; they serve because ministry flows from their hearts. They are not to assume leadership of the flock to attain authority and influence but because they are stewards of God's call on their lives. This call includes the entrustment of a sacred responsibility – the care of a congregation.

Pastor-leaders model ministry by example. They must never forget that care and nurture are not only indispensable but also biblical. As they seek to become more effective shepherds, reading, writing and memorising must be ministry lifestyle disciplines. They must be familiar with the great literature and resources available on pastoral ministry. Continuing to grow and develop must be a way of life. Yet leaders must remember the true sourcebook for ministry is the Word of God.

Jesus' encounter with Simon Peter in John 21 gives insight to those who have heard His call to care for His sheep and lambs.

> When they had finished eating, Jesus said to Simon Peter, 'Simon son of John, do you truly love me more than these?' 'Yes, Lord,' he said, 'you know that I love you.' Jesus said, 'Feed my lambs.' Again Jesus said, 'Simon son of John, do you truly love me?' He answered, 'Yes, Lord, you know that I love you.' Jesus said, 'Take care of my sheep.' The third time

he said to him, 'Simon son of John, do you love me?' Peter was hurt because Jesus asked him the third time, 'Do you love me?' He said, 'Lord, you know all things; you know that I love you.' Jesus said, 'Feed my sheep'. (vv. 15–17)

Peter responded to Christ's first query in the affirmative, telling the Lord that he loved Him. Christ followed up with a command – straightforward and direct: 'Feed my lambs.' Peter assumed it was now understood that he loved the Lord and that he was willing to carry out his nurturing responsibilities. Jesus asked Peter a second time, 'Do you truly love me?' His answer was the same: '[Of course,] you know that I love you.' '[If that is so,]' said Jesus, 'take care of my sheep.' Jesus asked Simon Peter a third time, 'Do you love me?' Simon grew frustrated. '[Of course, Jesus, you know everything]; you know that I love you.' '[Love requires action, Peter.] Feed my sheep.' Pastors with the ring of Christ's sheep-caring call in their souls step forth in ministry as channels of His nurture and love to His flock. Nurturing the congregation takes on the challenge of 'extending the Master Shepherd's heart and hand'.

Nurturing the Congregation

What is meant by the phrase 'nurturing the congregation'? Included in the concept is the role of 'pastoral care', but it involves more. Perhaps a more accurate description for contemporary church life is 'congregational care'. The nurturing ministries of a congregation entail far more than any person, no matter how gifted, can provide. Instead of the minister conceptualising the nurturing task as all his or her responsibility, the goal must be to mobilise the congregation to reach out in care and nurture – to each other and to needs outside their community of faith. The leader's objective then becomes developing 'ministers of care' who nurture and develop other nurturers until all members of the community of faith are equipped to reach to and care for family members, neighbours, and those in their sphere of daily interaction. The leader seeks to develop and cultivate a spirit, an aura, of nurture in the congregation that expresses itself in authentic ministry – both informal and structured. This spirit is fuelled by the Spirit of Christ in the hearts of believers who commune with Him and with each other.

The constraining love of Christ is the great motivator. Ministers filled with His love lead by example in loving people. Members of the faith community follow the lead of Christ and their minister in loving those who need their nurturing care.

Jesus said, 'I am the good shepherd; I know my sheep and my sheep know me ... My sheep listen to my voice; I know them, and they follow me' (John 10:14, 27).

Here is powerful pastoral imagery. The Good Shepherd knows His sheep. He nurtures them, speaks to them and cares for them in a manner that inspires them to follow Him. The Good Shepherd builds authentic, credible relationship with the sheep. The good pastoral undershepherd will likewise give attention to relationship building. There is no instantaneous way to know the sheep. Relationship building and nurturing require time. The goal of the undershepherd is to represent the Master Shepherd in a manner that inspires love, faith and discipleship to the Shepherd of all of the sheep.

Nurturing and the Community of Faith

Every member of the human family needs nurture and care. This is a basic need in each of our psyches. Many of the maladies of our day have as a root cause the lack of care and nurture. Nurturing is a part of the church's health. Since the church is a living organism, like all living things it should grow. The question, 'What will it take for our church to grow?' really should be, 'What obstacle is keeping our church from growing?' 'What do we need to replace or remove that will help our church regain its health and experience spiritual and numerical growth?'

What does a healthy, nurturing and caring church look like? There are many observable attributes of a church that is healthy:

- Healthy churches help everyone discover a sense of purpose, a purpose based on the Bible and God's plan for the ordering of life.

- Healthy churches create within their fellowship a place of belonging. People refer to the church as 'my' church and 'our' minister.

- Healthy churches intentionally seek to create an environment of trust, which goes a long way towards creating community.

- Healthy churches give ample and multiple opportunities to form relationships. They have found that creating many avenues of interaction is more likely to connect new people. They understand that the faithful in the congregation have relational waiting lists. These folks cannot possibly squeeze in one more relationship. So healthy churches offer small groups where new people can make friends with other new people.

- Healthy churches find ways to get as many people as possible involved in ministry. They understand that people who are actively engaged using their spiritual gifts will likely be more satisfied and feel a greater sense of community with the congregation.

- Healthy churches also understand the importance of keeping the vision and the mission before the people. They never assume that everyone buys into the mission. Every available means is used to constantly remind the people of who the church is and why it exists.

- Healthy churches also believe in constant training and equipping of their people. Training that equips not only reinforces the vision and mission but also creates a feeling of togetherness and cohesiveness. Giving people something to do and then not providing them the necessary tools or equipment leads to frustration and high turnover.

What is the local church to be about? The answer should be *the fulfilment of the Great Commission and the Great Commandment.* The local church is to be about fulfilling God's missional concern for our world, our community and our constituency. The church is to help God's people develop into strong Christ-followers who in turn join in fulfilling the Great Commission and the Great Commandment.

Vision aids the church to see the community of disciples God envisions and desires. The church, directed by Spirit-anointed servant-leaders, implements ministries designed to nurture and develop believers who desire to become completely devoted followers of Christ. This process requires growth and change. Change seldom is easy. But wholesome and godly change is worth the effort.

Pastors, by the nature of God's call on their lives, are agents of change. Pastoral ministry is complex. It requires a continual quest for what is right, what is excellent and what is God's will. Adjustments and improvement are components in this formula.

In this complicated world leaders and congregations may too easily settle for options that promise seemingly easy answers. At times the simplest path seems to be a new leader, a new programme or a new building. The objective, however, is to know God's will and way. Those who apply themselves to His way find understanding and grace for the fulfilment of ministry, even when the implementation is not easy.

The Importance of Relationships

For the better part of 20 years I served as a parish pastor. When I received my call to preach as a college student, I had no idea all that would be involved with saying yes to the call of God on my life. After leaving the local church pastorate to assume my present assignment, I realised just how much pastoring had become part of my DNA. Listening to the people of God pour out their stories of pain, defeat, joy, sadness, and a hundred other emotions, had become a way of life. Leading the same congregation had become a large part of my world. Astonishment overwhelmed me when I stepped into another ministry assignment. I have reflected and I found that what I miss most is the community and 'connectedness' that come through the leadership of the local church. Life looks quite different from this side of the altar.

When I served on the pastoral ministry side of the altar, I was impressed with preaching and music. These components of worship are not as impressive to me on this side of the altar. I now think I understand what new people experience when they take their place in the pew. Connection with people, relationships with others, is a major issue in congregational life.

God's design is that our faith will be lived out in community. Every person has been built with a need for love and nurture in community. The challenge of leader and people is to so winsomely represent the love and nurture of Christ in congregational care that the need for nurture is met in the authentic fellowship of the community of faith.

This translates into a simple but powerful focus statement for pastoral and congregational care: *Ministry is about people.*

Inherent in the statement is *need*. Needs range from those present by the fact of human existence, as identified by 'Maslow's Hierarchy of Need', to the range of specific needs that accumulate through everyday living. Numbers of people enter the doors of our churches and take their places on the pews with aching needs. Many have experienced broken relationships and are longing for relationships that are quality and whole. Numbers are discouraged. They are beaten down through the events and expressions of everyday life. Some are lacking direction, and still others are confused. All are needing to feel significant and loved. All want to know that they matter to God and to those who represent Him.

The community of faith becomes the community of hope. The church is the dispenser of grace, hope and redemption. Christ is the Hope, the Light, 'the way and the truth and the life' (John 14:6)! Christ through His people holds out the answers for needs, including the ultimate needs of life. The church's challenge is to lift a vision of the risen Christ – His grace, His will, His way – that will burn its way into the lives of questing hearts for eternity!

Pastoral care no longer assumes the minister is the sole caregiver. In today's culture, pastoral care involves and engages congregational care. The message of Christ, the Hope, is committed to faithful men and women who are challenged to 'pastorally' minister to the needs of those around them. The servant-leader identifies those in the congregation God has gifted with particular ministries and challenges them to 'carry the baton' in their area of gifting. Through this model the leader's ministry is duplicated. This approach, of course, involves training, organising and overseeing. The minister must 'educate' through preaching and teaching the biblical mandate that every believer is a minister of the message of Christ via the Great Commission. In the process, the minister will also see that the members and regular attendees are receiving nurture and care. Effective follow-up for first-time guests, as well as discipleship and assimilation, should all be a part of the overall ministry – organised in a manner so that the church is providing both nurture and care.

One key component of successful congregational ministry is assimilation. No matter how effective leader and people may be in winning new people to Christ and the church, follow-up that provides ample opportunities to become a part of the congregation's care network is vital. Each new person must experience a sense of belonging. By giving serious attention to assimilation, a minimal number of people will exit through the infamous 'back door'. They will 'connect' with someone who cares and will feel a part of the community. Beyond meeting their need for worship, their need for authentic fellowship will be met, and they will likely grow in relationship with Christ as well as with members in the faith fellowship.

At times a new calling or caring programme generates excitement. At first the new programme seems to take on a life of its own. People become enthused about the good things God is doing through the new ministry. Most organised programmes for caring, however, slowly lose momentum. How can this be avoided? One key lies in the continual incorporation of new people who have been reached and helped by the ministry. Recruiting the people new to the church must be the priority.

Small-group ministry is a 'connection' for people that has proven effective in numbers of outreaching, growing churches. These churches welcome an ever-increasing number of people who bring their personal needs, their need for relationships and their need for ministry. Numbers of small groups provide an environment where people can connect through care and relationships and be involved in ministry as well.

It is the case that at times the leader must provide encouragement and training for those who have caught the vision of the vast needs but who realise their inadequacy. These people sometimes feel that their ministry contribution won't make a dent in what needs to be accomplished. They feel overwhelmed. In every training and equipping programme in the church, there must be a clear biblical rationale for ministry and a vision of what really can be done for the cause of Christ. He is the enabler, the equipper of His people for ministry. Through His strength, His undershepherds can be challenged, inspired and empowered for their works of ministry. The minister is the leader in fostering an atmosphere of optimism for lay leaders who are reaching out and caring in the name of Christ, the Hope.

Each minister and congregation must work together to understand God's call and vision for them as a ministering body. The God of infinite variety knows the personality of each local community and the unique way it can connect people to people – within its fellowship and beyond. Organised approaches to care will be varied. Some will involve face-to-face contact. Some will use small groups that have a care/nurture application. Relationships will at times develop through networks and support groups. Ministry to people will involve listening as well as speaking. The building and nurturing of *relationships* around the all-caring and nurturing centre of Christ is the key. And His illuminating and empowering grace is the fuel that drives the vehicle of ministry.

Pastor, leader, let me encourage you. You may not be able to craft and deliver a sermon like a bishop, but you can love, care for and create an enriching environment of nurture for your people. Your choir may not deliver the polished music of studio recordings, but your people can be trained to love, encourage, befriend and disciple the new ones God sends to your congregation. Church is still about connections. It's about family connections – connecting people to our heavenly Father and connecting them to those He calls His children.

There is no greater reward than the joy of knowing we are fulfilling the Father's purpose as we minister in His name. Pastor, as you lead your people to experience this joy, both you and they will delight in the greatest fulfilment of all – meeting the needs of others and enjoying the Father's smile!

For Further Reading

Adsit, Christopher B., *Personal Disciple Making*. San Bernardino, Calif.: Here's Life Publishing, 1988.

Anderson, Leith, *Leadership That Works*. Minneapolis: Bethany House Publishing House, 1999.

Anderson, Lynn, *They Smell Like Sheep*. West Monroe, La.: Howard Publishing Co., 1997.

Barna, George, *User Friendly Churches*. Ventura, Calif.: Gospel Light, 1991.

Blackaby, Henry, and Richard, *Spiritual Leadership*. Nashville: Broadman and Holman, 2001.

Cook, Jerry, with Stanley Baldwin, *Love, Acceptance, and Forgiveness*. Ventura, Calif.: Gospel Light, 1979.

Cueni, R. Robert, *What Ministers Can't Learn in Seminary*. Nashville: Abingdon, 1988.

Dale, Robert D., *Leading Edge*. Nashville: Abingdon, 1996.

Fisher, David, *The 21st Century Pastor*. Grand Rapids: Zondervan, 1996.

George, Carl F., *Prepare Your Church for the Future*. Grand Rapids: Baker Book House, 1991.

Greenleaf, Robert K., *The Power of Servant Leadership*. San Francisco: Berrett-Koehler, 1998.

Larson, Bruce, Paul Anderson, and Doug Self, *Mastering Pastoral Care*. Portland Oreg.: Multnomah, 1990.

Oster, Merrill, *Vision-Driven Leadership*. San Bernardino, Calif.: Here's Life Publishing, 1991.

Smith, Harold Ivan, *When Your People Are Grieving*. Kansas City: Beacon Hill Press, 2001.

Yancey, Philip, *Church: Why Bother?* Grand Rapids: Zondervan, 1999.

Neil B. Wiseman, PhD, served as academic dean and professor of pastoral development at Nazarene Bible College in Colorado Springs. He has served Christ and the Church as a pastor, professor, author, editor and conference leader. His published works include *The Untamed God: Unleashing the Supernatural in the Body of Christ*, *The Heart of a Great Pastor: How to Grow Strong and Thrive Wherever God Has Planted You* (with H.B. London), and *They Call Me Pastor: How to Love the Ones You Lead* (with H.B. London). Neil and his wife, Bonnie, make their home in Overland Park, Kansas.

New Paradigms for Pastoral Care

NEIL B. WISEMAN

Agape energises ministry and empowers the Jesus leadership style. When this two-way love flows between pastor and people, ministry seems to be the most satisfying of all vocations. Then molehills don't become mountains and expectations don't frustrate. But if love is missing, ministry becomes a lot like an old country doctor making dutiful rounds without medicine.

I have believed for more years than I care to count that the most beautiful words in any language are 'love' and 'pastor'. The meaning and feelings embedded in those two words are among my most treasured memories of representing Jesus in the crises of my parishioners' lives.

Being a pastor – or as it was called in an earlier century, a physician of souls – is what I was born to be. My years of leading a congregation provided rich privileges as people opened their lives to me. In my teaching years, I viewed myself as a pastor on loan who had the magnificent opportunity of multiplying my ministry through students.

These pastoral-heart expressions bring me to this concept: Being a pastor or minister is something you are much more than something you do. Its loftiest responsibilities are speaking for God in the pulpit and representing God to folks in their times of need – a presence, a caring and a nearness rolled into comfort for the parishioner and satisfaction for the minister.

The need for loving ministers has never been more urgent than now. In a high-tech and low-touch society, millions feel isolated, lonely and hungry for closer human relationships. Some do not even realise their inner emptiness results from being so disconnected. With the two-parent family in decline, thousands – maybe millions – need God's family more than ever now. In our highly mobile society, many live miles away from their extended families, so children grow up without the affirmation and affection of grandparents, aunts and uncles.

And what about times when pain and ambiguities come? Many who need a pastor most are those facing their first crisis. A wise old preacher advised me years ago, 'An ounce of heartache or one serious illness makes people think seriously about God, but they likely will not do much about Him without a pastor to help them.'

Still another reason for giving priority to pastoral care and contacts is because every dimension of ministry is for people. Preaching, administration, worship leadership, compassion, evangelism and counselling are all about people – how they think, how they act and how they feel. So to miss pastoral care is to lose touch with those who are the focus of ministry. I am willing to say without hesitation, 'Ministers who do not keep close to people soon lose the edge and meaning of all other phases of ministry.'

In spite of these pressing needs, the relational dimensions of pastoral ministry are under assault these days. Some reasons are obvious; others, more subtle. Confusion reigns. And some ministers have stopped trying. Though we have problems, one irreducible reality remains – we cannot abandon pastoral care and people contact and still call ourselves pastors. To bring light to the discussion, I want to share what I have been hearing and thinking about the contemporary status of the relational dimensions of ministry.

What a Hospital Bed Taught Me

I gained fresh insight about ministry two summers ago from a hospital bed. Something strange happened to me at two o'clock one morning in a motel room, miles from home. My heart didn't feel right – no pain, just a heaviness.

I didn't know what to do – this medical stuff was outside my personal experience. I had never had surgery, had infrequent visits to doctors, and had spent only one night in a hospital for tests. But my recalling all those graphic TV warnings about heart attacks made me decide I needed to be checked.

So I woke my wife, Bonnie, and said something like, 'Don't worry, but I need to go to the emergency room.'

'Don't worry,' she responded as we dressed, dashed for the car and sped eight miles to the hospital.

Chest discomfort gets quick attention in emergency rooms. Soon I had medical types probing and questioning and writing and testing and whispering to each other.

'What's wrong?' I asked and received only a vague word or two for an answer.

Finally the doctor said, 'You will have to stay.'

'What's wrong, and for how long?' I asked again.

His answer was, 'Maybe nothing but maybe something. We need more tests.'

Since I am a champion melancholic worrier, questions cascaded like Niagara Falls through my mind. Did I have unfinished business with my wife, children or God? Would my grandchildren come to a solid faith without me? Did I have the dying grace I preached for years? And the most amusing question of all was, 'Will anybody come to my funeral?' From 2am until dawn allowed plenty of time for asking my questions over and over.

Then everything changed – dramatically. About 7:15am, veteran pastor Norm Rickie, himself in need of hip surgery, limped into my room. He pulled a chair next to my bed so his eyes met mine and said, 'I've come to pray with you. It's your time to receive ministry.'

As he quoted Romans 8:28 and prayed for me by name, my room was transformed into a place of peace. When he finished praying, a strange sentence of gratitude tumbled from my lips: 'Though I never thought of you as handsome, you look more like Jesus than anyone I ever saw.' We both laughed at my words, but we knew we had had a meeting with the Holy One.

My lesson – in times of trouble, pastoral care is more important than able-bodied ministers realise. Or maybe a more specific way to state my discovery would be – every minister needs a health crisis so he or she can fully understand the significance of pastoral care.

What I Am Learning from Pastors

Over a two- or three-year period, I have been resource leader in 20 pastors' retreats. These events offer opportunities for dialogue with ministers who tell me keeping in touch with people is harder now than ever before. Vast changes in family, school, work and culture cause scheduling problems. Husband and wife are both employed outside the home. Evenings and weekends are full. Getting into most people's schedule is so difficult that it's easy to just give up trying.

Meanwhile, the questions of caring relationships between minister and people keep coming up at pastors' conferences and in conversations with key laypersons. Apparently, close contact between believers and their spiritual leader is considered to be highly desirable by congregants as well as by ministers.

Though the difficulties are real, they are not insurmountable. Since we cannot give up the relational dynamics of ministry, I plead for tough-minded thinking to develop innovative ways to accomplish the goals of touching people for Christ.

As a start towards solving the problem, I want to state my basic assumption that frequent casual contacts build relational bridges over which the minister walks to serve people in crises. For purpose of clarity, I am using the term 'pastoral contact' as any meeting of a minister with another person in any setting, whether by chance or by formal arrangement. This contact concept offers a way for a pastor to be close enough to spot more serious needs that people are experiencing and at the same time provides a sense of connectedness so a parishioner feels free to ask for greater assistance when it is needed.

In his hard-hitting, insightful book, *Jesus the Pastor*, John W. Frye helps us refocus our understanding of the pastor's work: 'Our common English word pastor has made its way to us through Latin and is simply the semantic equivalent of the biblical word for shepherd ... The term pastor (shepherd) may be gutted of value in our culture (even in the evangelical culture), but never is it downplayed by Jesus or the New Testament writers. Jesus Christ is the supreme Shepherd and the ultimate Senior Pastor.'[1]

Like a thundering prophet calling us back to first things, Frye continues: 'As the pastoral vocation teeters on the brink of this new millennium, churches and the world will increasingly need undershepherds who are less like each other and increasingly more like Jesus, the Chief Shepherd.'[2]

What I Have Learned from Scripture

Revisit with me a well-known conversation between Jesus and Peter (see John 21). Listen to impulsive Peter's frustration as Jesus teaches him lessons he would never forget. Our Lord asks Peter three times, 'Do you love me?' Three times Peter replied, 'You know I love you.' Each time our Lord gives a clear directive planned to shape Peter's ministry: 'Feed my lambs', 'Care for my sheep', and 'Feed my sheep'.

Of the passage, William Barclay commented so warmly, 'Peter might not write and think like John; he might not voyage and adventure like Paul; but *he had the great honour, and the lovely task, of being the shepherd of the sheep of Christ.*'[3]

Later, after many years of growing his soul and maturing his ministry, Peter testified to ministers in all generations, including ours: 'Here's my concern: that *you care for God's flock with all the diligence of a shepherd.* Not because you have to, but because you want to please God. Not calculating what you can get out of it, but acting spontaneously. Not bossily telling others what to do, but tenderly showing them the way' (1 Pet. 5:1–3, *The Message*, emphasis added).

Love overflowed from his agape-filled heart when Paul wrote to the church at Thessalonica that he ministered to them 'like a mother caring for her little children' and a father 'encouraging, comforting and urging' his children 'to live lives worthy of God' (1 Thess. 2:7, 11–12).

Jesus, Peter and Paul make it crystal clear that a pastor's love for God is measured by how well the sheep under his or her care are tended and fed.

What I Don't Want to Learn from Rumours and Hearsay

The following reports were told to me by persons whose veracity I trust completely. I hope they are not true, but I am afraid they are.

Church No. 1. I received a postcard from a retired district superintendent that makes this request: 'You remember my sister – you used to be her pastor. She is all alone and lives in a small room in a rest home in the town where you teach. I visited her the other day, and she said someone from the church comes once a year to visit and serve Communion at Thanksgiving. She thinks she is dying and asked me to write to see if you would have her funeral when she dies. She worries that the ministers at her church will be too busy to bury her.'

Church No. 2. Go to another setting where a grisly old rancher, a member of one church for 45 years, lived alone following the death of his wife. After he was diagnosed with a terminal illness, he checked himself into a hospice. The pastoral staff called once in the five weeks it took him to die. During that time, he phoned a former pastor to ask if he would have his funeral because 'I don't want someone to say nice things about me when I am dead who couldn't come to say a short prayer for me when I was alive.'

Church No. 3. A founder member of a church in a large city has been away from God for years. Now she has terminal cancer and calls the church. She explains her previous connection and requests someone to come and pray with her. The person who answers the church phone replies, 'We don't do that around here. I suggest you call the cancer society.'

Perhaps these incidents may be a bit overstated, but they all point to malfeasance of duty by the undershepherd. E. Glenn Wagner, in his epic book *Escape from Church, Inc.,* put the axe to the root of our contemporary problem: 'Until we embrace the relational aspects of knowing God and his heart, until we learn both to challenge and to encourage one another to deeper levels of interaction, we will never get to the human heart. We will spend our lives merely living by the rules.'[4]

Unpacking the Difficulties and Confusion

The dilemma ministers face is how to maintain or improve close ties with their people given their present situations, their own busy lives and the whirlwind lifestyles of so many of their people. Solutions must be found. To help us unpack the problems, I propose revisiting several bedrock foundational aspects of pastoral care and contact.

1. The Priority Self-Care Factor. Everyone's life consists of 168 hours per week, no matter their age, job or geography. How we use our hours determines our effectiveness and our awareness of whether or not we are fulfilling God's plan.

Let's admit that killing stress has deep roots in three factors: an uncritical acceptance of executive/leadership duties, the myth of ministerial invincibility, and/or a faulty belief that outside forces write our schedules. Of course, the leader's self-care and soul health, as H.B. London and I have discussed in depth in other places, must be written into every leader's time allocation plan. Stress, overload, hurry and no time off will make you ill, shorten your life and short-circuit your ministry.

Thus the newer paradigms of pastoral care and contact are not intended to be added to a minister's schedule. Rather, they are to replace some things he or she is doing. Actually, this is a call to relinquish other areas of ministry to see that prayer, sermon preparation and people contact have the highest priorities. To amplify good guidance from Kirk B. Jones's book, *Rest in the Storm*, we must confess, confront and correct self-violence.[5] Something has to go, but it cannot be preaching or pastoral care.

2. The Incarnational Factor. Authentic pastoral care follows the Jesus incarnational-shepherd model. And of course, the biggest need of all is for a healthy soul and a sound relationship with the Lord. The holy nearness for which I plead releases in the minister an extraordinary compassion, increased spiritual savvy, authentic new ways of seeing, empowered ways of being and divinely energised ways of doing. Then ministry becomes excitingly effective because of the One who is helping us.

3. The People Factor. Two sentences from Leonard Griffith's masterful book published a generation ago remind us, 'We need to soak our souls in the priorities of Jesus and be reminded constantly that persons come first. Our ministries are made for persons, not persons for our ministry.'[6]

Now as always, people are the church's reason for being. Caring for straying people stands at the heart of the Bible story (see Matt. 18:12–14) about the shepherd who left the ninety-nine to go to the treacherous hillsides to search for the one lost sheep – a perfect example of the ministry model of Jesus.

4. The Informational Factor. Pastoral care informs preaching – then our sermons are turned into actual messages for real people we serve. Without firsthand involvement in the details of living and dying, preaching becomes remote, perfunctory, irrelevant and even inane.

What we preach, how we preach and how our preaching is received are all greatly influenced by what we know about people. Authority for preaching comes from our call and accurate communication of Scripture. But knowing people and loving them – warts and all – makes preaching pertinent and useful.

5. The Critical-Time Factor. Reluctant, halfhearted, or late response to a pressing personal need always undermines the effectiveness of pastoral care. Be quick to respond to crises and transitions in the lives of your congregants. When you arrive to help them with one of these difficulties, pray with the persons in need and stay long enough to show your care. Don't overtalk and don't try to explain the unexplainable.

The list of crises and transition opportunities include the birth of a child, vocational promotion or demotion, divorce, child leaving home, hospital experience, emotional problems, conversion, marriage, retirement, new obligation for aged parents, death in the family, significant celebrations, disasters and misunderstandings in the church.

6. The Victory Factor. A highly significant function of pastoral care is to communicate the good news that victory is possible for the child of God. Go back a few years with me to Vanderbilt University Hospital in Nashville. Jim Sankey, on the pastoral team for some years, is showing the ropes about hospital calling to Karen Dean (now Karen Dean Fry), the new college-age pastor. One sentence in their conversation establishes him as a true shepherd: 'Karen, one of our church staff calls every day on the sick and dying because they are the ones the devil attacks first.'

7. The Spiritual-Health-of-Leaders Factor. Ministry to the strong keeps a church healthy and provides a minister with partners in ministry. Leaders, longtime Christians and those who seem to be spiritually strong may be hurting or fighting some inner battle where they need a pastor.

One good way to deliver pastoral care to leaders is to develop the decision-making group of your church into a microcosm of what you want the church to be. You can use Acts 4:32–35 as your pattern. One veteran minister said as he started retirement, 'If I were starting over, I would have board meetings every month but deal with administrative issues every other month and personal spiritual development on the alternate months. I believe my board meetings would have been shorter and better focused. Then a spirit of cooperation and goodwill and modeling the spirit of Jesus will develop across the entire congregation.'

Strategies Any Pastor Can Use

From the first word of this chapter, I have been subtly asking whether pastoral care is harder now or whether the problem is that we are glad to have an excuse not to try to do pastoral care anymore. If you have a problem doing pastoral care because of logistics and the changing culture, I plan to offer several ways of how to do it well in our time.

What strategies will work in our day? And whenever I use the word 'strategies', I am reminded of my old friend, Dr R.W. Cunningham, who enjoyed telling me, 'Any plan will work if we work it.'

1. Use the pastoral-care spectrum. I have listed the chart below, but let me explain its meaning and usefulness.

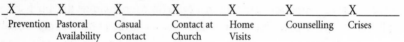

X	X	X	X	X	X	X
Prevention	Pastoral Availability	Casual Contact	Contact at Church	Home Visits	Counselling	Crises

The idea is that every phase of ministry on the chart delivers pastoral care, and the ministries get more intense as you move towards the right. Starting on the left of the graph is 'prevention', which means classes, seminars and study groups on subjects such as basic Christianity, marriage and parenting. Move then to the 'casual contact' in the community and in church. Next is 'home visits', as invited or needed – it is doubtful that you can really know other persons until you have seen them in their home settings. When more serious difficulties arise, the pastor may provide 'pastoral counselling' or refer the person to a competent counsellor. At the extreme right, in times of 'crises', the pastor offers the greatest amount of support and pastoral care.

2. Search your heart to see if God can trust you with more people.

Recently, I had a stimulating conversation with a minister who, with his mission-minded congregation, has resurrected a dying church in a neighbouring town. His church gave people, prayer, affection, money and work teams to refurbish the building. When I inquired what it was like those first few weeks the core people for the new church were gone, he replied, 'The Lord has helped us replace the people we gave.'

Then he said something I can't forget: 'God will give a church as many people as He can trust them to care for.' If he is right, the effectiveness of our evangelism is at least partially determined by the quality of the pastoral care we provide.

3. Train laity to do pastoral care. Dale Galloway clarifies the issues like this: 'Pastoral care, a biblical expectation and a human need, cannot be abandoned because a church gets too large or the work too time consuming. The true shepherds never get away from the desire to be involved with the people God entrusts to them. But pastoral care can be effectively shared with laity. Your church has many wonderful caregivers who will do this ministry well after they are given basic training. Pastoral care has to be done, but it does not all have to be done by the senior minister.'[7] In Galloway's book, *Building Teams in Ministry*, he says the key issues regarding training laypersons to do pastoral care are ongoing training, specific assignments and regular reporting. Laypersons cannot do all the pastoral care that is needed, but they can do much of it.

4. Use traditional methods if they work in your setting. Here's a surprising fact – sociologists say as many as 25 per cent of people are at home during the day. That means 25 per cent of all pastoral contacts could be made during the day when most of us believe no one is available. Then, too, the housebound are glad for pastoral care anytime. Don't give up on any method that is working in your setting.

5. Contact as many people as possible at church. In small to middle-sized churches, that means everyone. Greet people before the service, after the service and during the family-of-God time. In conversation, add a pastoral touch such as, 'How are you doing spiritually?' 'I prayed for you this week.' Or 'I'm counting on you to pray for me while I preach this morning.' Make eye contact and touch people.

Consider praying for people at the open altar as you would in a healing service by touching them as you pray for them by name.

One minister I know invites visitors and needy people to meet him at the front of the sanctuary following the service. He takes time to pray for each individual. He gives each visitor a New Testament. In fact, he makes a minipastoral call on each individual right there. And all who look on are impressed by his care for people and sense he will be there for them in their time of need.

6. Use the phone creatively. Make it a point to call 10 people every day; it can be done in 30 minutes. If you reach a recording, express your care with a comment such as, 'The Lord brought you to my mind this morning, and I just wanted to tell you that I prayed for you today.'

Some people can be phoned at their place of employment with a brief word such as, 'I was thinking about you this morning. Do you have a minute for me to have a brief prayer with you right now?'

Even the busiest minister can call 10 visitors in half an hour. The message goes like this: 'This is Pastor/Reverend Tom Brown. I want to thank you for coming to our church today. Tell me about yourself. And can I pray for you before we hang up – I'll just take a minute.' One older pastor who phones visitors on Sunday afternoon won a couple who visited and later led both sets of their parents and two of their grown siblings and their young families to Christ.

7. Use snail mail. Hand-addressed first-class mail always gets read. A handwritten note impacts the receiver way out of proportion to the effort it requires. As a pastor, I tried to write at least 10 short notes on Sunday afternoon to thank people for ministry that morning. Some people kept those notes for years.

Two business people used notes to make me a repeat customer. One was a real estate agent who remembered to write to my wife and me on our birthdays and on the anniversary of the day she sold us our home. Naturally, when we decided to change houses again, she was the first agent that came to our minds. A similar experience came from a car purchase. Our salesman sent birthday cards and personal notes plus called long distance at two-month intervals to see how the car was working. Needless to say, I have bought two cars from him, and though I have moved a thousand miles from him, he recently called to tell me he would deliver the kind of car I wanted when I was ready to purchase another one.

8. Use email creatively. Almost everyone either has an email address or is about to get one. You can arrange to send messages to a master list so they all hear from you within a brief period of time. Only your imagination limits what you can do with email.

9. Contact everyone regularly. With a bit of organised effort, everyone can be contacted every month, especially in the smaller churches. Perhaps once a month is too much to expect in larger churches, but maybe not. One Southeast Asian Church of the Nazarene in California grew rapidly to over 500 because they had a phone bank system at the church where everyone – members as well as prospects – were called and prayed with by phone every Saturday. One Saturday morning, I saw 20 persons making calls and praying with people by phone.

10. Use the ripple effect for finding prospects. The way this concept works is to contact people directly but disarm them by saying, 'I'm in the ministry to help as many people as possible. Do you know anyone who needs a pastor to help them or pray with them?'

In the conversation they will tell you about someone who needs help. Be prepared to follow up on the lead they give. Often before the conversation ends, they admit they have a personal need. Be sure to give them your business card so they can call you when they think of others who need you.

The ripple effect can be used in door-to-door calling, in general hospital calling, in conversation with persons who share a hospital room with one of your parishioners or even with people you meet through business contacts.

One church planter set up a drink stand outside the main door of a large appartment block. Some people stood around to talk, which gave him opportunity to use the ripple effect questions. Naturally, he became the talk of the residents, some of whom became prospects for his church.

Every person you meet – saint or sinner – has a network of persons who need the Lord. When he or she learns you are trustworthy, he or she will tell you about their needy friends and relatives. Those who give you names of friends may never respond to your ministry, but someone from the network of friends and relatives will.

Take God to the People
I borrowed this simple sentence from John W. Frye: 'Pastoring means taking God to the people.' When I muse on that idea, I move from the world of the study and pulpit to the world of harassed, weary people to help them experience Immanuel – God with us. And I joyously commit anew every detail of ministry to my Senior Pastor, Jesus.

Notes
1. John W. Frye, *Jesus the Pastor* (Grand Rapids: Zondervan Publishing House, 2000), 18.
2. Ibid., 19.
3. William Barclay, *The Gospel of John*, vol. 2 in *The Daily Bible Study Series* (Philadelphia: The Westminster Press, 1955), 332.
4. E. Glenn Wagner, *Escape from Church, Inc.* (Grand Rapids: Zondervan Publishing House, 1999), 201.

5. Kirk Byron Jones, *Rest in the Storm* (Valley Forge, Pa.: Judson Press, 2001), 9.

6. Leonard Griffith, *We Have This Ministry* (Waco, Tex.: Word Books, 1973), 37.

7. Dale Galloway, *Building Teams in Ministry* (Kansas City: Beacon Hill Press of Kansas City, 2000), 24.

Jim Pettitt, PhD, serves as co-ordinator of Family and Men's Ministries for the Church of the Nazarene. Prior to this assignment, he served 17 years as a pastor. He also served as adjunct professor of pastoral care and counselling at Nazarene Theological Seminary. Jim and his wife, Jeanette Downs Pettitt, travel doing Nazarene Marriage Enrichment seminars throughout the United States. The Downs live in Olathe, Kansas.

Fundamentals of Pastoral Counselling

JIM PETTITT

Praise be to the God and Father of our Lord Jesus Christ,
the Father of compassion and the God of all comfort, who comforts
us in all our troubles, so that we can comfort those in any trouble
with the comfort we ourselves have received from God.
2 Cor. 1:3–4

'Pastoral counselling' is an important part of ministry. While their primary call is to mediate the relationship between God and parishioners, more often pastors, or ministers, find themselves mediating human relationships and the relationships of parishioners with their problems. This is consistent with Scripture, that is, the second great commandment to love your neighbour (wife, husband, child, fellow parishioner, etc.), which is inseparably linked to the first, to love God (see Matt. 22:37–40). To ignore the second is to diminish the first. If pastors want to teach others to love God, they must also deal with human relationships, and from these relationships flow most of the problems faced by their parishioners.

Ministers find themselves in a peculiar and most effective position to become counsellors to their people. Edwin Friedman suggests four reasons why the pastoral counsellor has this unique and effective access to people's lives. First, the minister has access to the history of the family. The potential information to be gained from this history can be invaluable in assessing the situation. Second, the minister often has access to individuals and families during public and private rites of passage (weddings, funerals, dedications and baptisms) and often directs these rites of passage for the family. This intimate relationship provides ample opportunities to reach into lives and deal with problems and relationships at a time when the parishioner and family are most vulnerable and accepting. Third is the length of time over which the pastor has opportunity to know and become close with the congregational (and community) members. And finally, the members of the congregation look upon the minister as their leader. This leadership is seldom limited to spiritual matters, no matter how much the minister might wish it. That leadership must also address relational problems within the congregational family, within the families of the congregation, and the individual difficulties that flow from those relationships.[1]

David Dillon suggests three more practical reasons why counselling is an inevitable part of the pastoral ministry: availability, respectability and affordability. Pastors are often the most accessible and most visible among the helping professionals in the community. In addition, their positions as spiritual leaders bring to their counsel a sense of authority and respectability that is not found among other counsellors. And, more often than not, their advice and counsel is free. For those without insurance, on limited budgets, or with no experience in the realm of counselling, this is often the most important reason for choosing this avenue for help.[2]

This combination often marks the pastoral counsellor as the first choice for many in the congregation and community. The question is not *if* pastors will counsel, but *how* and *how much* they will make counselling a part of their ministries.

What Is Pastoral Counselling?

Perhaps pastoral counselling should first be defined by what it is not. To begin with, it is not professional psychotherapy. Ministers should not be involved in the diagnosis or treatment of psychological pathologies unless they have professional training in this area. This should be left to the professional therapist, psychologist or psychiatrist trained in such treatment.

The question then becomes, 'What are the responsibilities of a counselling minister?' James Hamilton suggests that at the very least (and yet most important of all) the counsellor should attempt 'to develop in individuals a relationship with God which gives access to the spiritual resources that flow from Him'.[3] Through prayer and the Word of God, great healing power can be experienced in the worst of situations, often bringing hope and wisdom beyond the counsellor's competence.

Friedman suggests that pastoral counselling is not just packaging psychology in Scripture. What makes pastoral counselling pastoral is 'whether or not we, as pastors, have listened to Scripture'.[4] The pastors take their own experiences with the healing Word and share those with hurting individuals, opening the door for God to work His will in their lives. David Benner suggests that the essence of counselling is not so much in what the counsellors do as in who the counsellors are and how they offer themselves to the person seeking help. Pastoral counsellors are to help 'people understand their problems and their lives in the light of their relationship to God'.[5]

Everett Worthington delineates four distinct requirements for counselling to be considered Christian (and therefore pastoral) counselling.

- The counselling must be consistent with the Christian assumptions (doctrinal, ethical and moral beliefs) the church holds as important.

- Such counselling must be consistent with God's revelation (Scripture).

- Such counselling must be done by a Christian person, not just a person who is sympathetic with Christian beliefs.

- Christ must be at the centre of the counselling process.[6]

Melvin Blanchette believes that counselling ministers should be those who clearly walk with their parishioners to a place of freedom, where they will be enabled to make healthy decisions for their lives.[7]

David Olson and John DeFrain theorise that leading individuals towards health can be as effective as leading them away from dysfunction.[8] This method is suited to pastoral ministry.[9] In many cases, ministers who help their parishioners learn to communicate, problem solve, spend time together in family relationships, be affirming and affectionate, understand God's unconditional love and do other relational and spiritual skills will be effective in their counselling ministry.

Consultation

Leaders should familiarise themselves with the resources available in the community and take advantage of those resources when needed. When facing an especially challenging counselling dilemma – one where the problem is not easily determined, or the counselling process gets stuck – consultation with a professional might be prudent. It is important to remember, however, that such resource persons maintain rigorous schedules and should be approached in a professional manner. In most cases, remuneration for services is expected. The professional may volunteer to donate services, but it is not appropriate to ask him or her to do so; otherwise the fee must be paid by the church or by the counsellee. Many churches have benevolent funds available for such instances.

Resources in the community might include the following:

- The medical community (doctors, nurses, hospitals, clinics)
- Social workers (social service providers)
- Mental health professionals (counsellors, psychologists, psychiatrists)
- Addiction counsellors
- Financial advisors
- Pregnancy crisis counsellors
- National hot lines maintained by such entities as Focus on the Family

An additional resource often overlooked is the clergy groups to which the minister may belong. The wealth of experience via fellow clergy can be a source of practical information and guidance.

When the minister decides to consult with another person, the permission issue comes into focus. When the problem or case is presented only in the most general terms, and there is no likelihood that the counsellee's identity might be disclosed, then no permission is needed. In the event, however, it is necessary to give particulars regarding that person's situation and there is some likelihood his or her identity could become known, the minister should let the person know about the consultation process ahead of time and secure in writing his or her permission to consult. Written permission should include the name of the consultant, his or her professional expertise, the exact parameters of the information to be shared, the signatures of the counsellee and the pastor, and the date.

Referral

Ministers might ask, 'When and why should I refer the individual or family to a professional?' The first and most obvious answer would be to refer whenever the counselling situation reveals a problem that is more complex than the training and ability of the pastoral counsellor. One pastor may refer every person who comes with problems that go beyond 'spiritual counselling', while another may choose to deal with relational and family problems but draws the line when psychological problems surface. Pastors without a graduate degree in a specific counselling area should refrain from dealing with psychological pathology, leaving such counselling to trained and licensed professionals.

A second reason ministers might 'pass' on a counselling situation is for contextual reasons. That is, pastors would want to avoid counselling situations that would put their positions as pastors and spiritual leaders of the church in jeopardy. In fact, some research suggests that nearly all nonspiritual counselling that extends into the private lives of individuals creates such jeopardy.[10] The pastor will often find it necessary to work with the individual or family on several levels, including at worship, in friendship and social situations, on committees and at official church functions. Knowing that the pastor is aware of intimate (and sometimes embarrassing) situations can create a level of discomfort the parishioner may not be able to overcome. One pastor stated that counselling even interfered with his freedom to preach on certain texts. More than one family left the church after expressing concern that he was preaching directly at them from his knowledge of their private situation. This is precisely the reason why mental health professionals are ethically forbidden to interact with their clients in any relationship beyond that of counsellor/client. For the pastor, this would seem to be unavoidable.

Counselling on sexual matters almost guarantees contextual conflict. The rule is to refer, refer and refer. Sexual issues should always be left to a professional counsellor or physician trained in those matters. A minister can simply reply to the raising of such issues by stating, 'I am not trained in these areas, and it would be inappropriate for me to deal with them as your pastor.' Much better to have them a little 'miffed' at this refusal than to enter into a situation that has destroyed more than one ministry and even some churches.

The final reason for referral is the time factor. If allowed, counselling can easily displace other equal or more important functions. There are simply more hurting people than there are hours in the day to deal with them. David Benner gives three important suggestions at this point.

First, ministers should set a limit on the hours of counselling done each week, balancing those hours against other duties such as sermon preparation and administration. It is easy to get caught up in the gratification of such a healing ministry, but the time invested must be kept in perspective to the minister's ministry as a whole.

Second, ministers should consider limiting themselves to doing short-term counselling, with goals that are attainable in a three- to four-session time frame. Problems that continue beyond that frame are probably better dealt with by professionals.[11]

Third, ministers may want to limit their counselling to congregational members or those in regular attendance. This suggestion speaks to possible liability and insurance issues and would certainly have some effect in limiting the counselling load. This does not mean that if someone from the community suddenly appears with a crisis situation, that he or she is ignored. It is always appropriate to address the crisis and lower the anxiety level. This can usually be done in one session. A referral at this point would be in order, with the minister doing ongoing spiritual counselling.[12]

Types of Mental Health Professionals. There are several types of mental health professionals (MHP) to whom the pastor can refer. Choosing the right one is an important part of pastoral counselling.

Clinical or counselling psychologists are trained in the assessment and treatment of psychological disorders, testing and assessment, and individual and group therapy. In the process of dealing with individual therapy, they often do marital and family therapy. The therapy, however, is still usually done from the individual point of view.

Psychiatrists are medical doctors with an additional three to four years of training in the treatment of psychological disorders. They often approach counselling from a medical point of view and lean towards medication for treatment. Many psychiatrists today limit their practice to prescribing medications, allowing other professionals to do the clinical therapy.

Social workers are usually trained in dealing with complex system problems, especially those arising from social issues such as poverty, crime, abuse and cultural issues. Their expertise in linking persons to services in the community can be very helpful in getting parishioners the help they need.

Counsellors (marriage and family therapists, licensed professional counsellors) deal with career issues, adjustment issues, relationships (marriage, family, friendship, etc), and general mental health difficulties (eg, depression, anger, grief).

Creating a Referral Network. One of the easiest ways for pastors to begin building their referral networks is to seek recommendations from fellow pastors, doctors and members of their parishes. Satisfied clients often (but not always) mean good practitioners and can cut the discovery process time considerably.

Once a list of professionals is created, the second step is to interview them in person. These interviews are important for several reasons and should be very specific in what they cover.

● They should reveal the types of services provided (marriage, family, individual, medication, etc).

● They should include questions regarding where the counsellors stand on Christian values and faith commitment. Will they respect the religious beliefs of the clients referred?

- They should reveal professional expertise. How long have the interviewees been practising, and what fields of expertise do they have? Where did they train? What are their professional affiliations? Do they have networking relationships with other professionals, clinics and hospitals in the area? What do they charge?

- They should help pastors to gain some subjective information, such as the professionals' interpersonal skills, whether they can get along with the client, and whether the pastor will feel comfortable working with them.

- They should indicate whether the professionals are willing to work with referring pastors in the healing process. This should include agreement on what legal releases may be required in this sharing process.

- And they should deal with the stand of the MHP on specific ethical issues of importance to referring pastors and their denominations, such as abortion, homosexuality, divorce and remarriage, and extramarital relationships.

These interviews should be seen as vitally important to the referral process. Research studies show that a client's personal values (including religious and faith values) are likely to change during the course of counselling and that that change will be towards the values that the counsellor holds.[13] The vulnerability of the counselling process and the faith the counsellee must place in the counsellor for effective results make this almost inevitable.

What about referrals to non-Christian professionals? While a Christian MHP would be preferable, there are two reasons why ministers might want to refer to non-Christian professionals. First, the Christian professional may not be as competent as other non-Christian professionals. Second, there may not be a Christian MHP available. In such cases, the interview process becomes an even more important safety measure.

When pastors decide to refer a parishioner to an MHP, there are six important steps to take:

1. Know the mental health professional (from recommendations and interviews).
2. Present the referral to the counsellee in an appropriate and professional manner.
3. Explain to the counsellee how to get in touch with the MHP and what to

expect regarding cost and process. In some cases, it may be appropriate for the pastor to make the appointment, but only with the knowledge and permission (written) of the counsellee.

4. Reassure the counsellee that this will not adversely affect the pastor-parishioner relationship. They often need to be assured that the referral is not a rejection.
5. Continue to maintain a close relationship with the counsellee, encouraging him or her emotionally and spiritually in the healing process.
6. Keep proper and regular contact with the MHP (to the extent he or she is willing to allow this to happen).[14]

Pastors who learn the value of consultation and careful and thoughtful referral will earn the gratitude of their congregational members and greatly enhance their own counselling and healing capabilities.

Counselling Ethics and Liability

Ethical Issues. The ethical issues involved in pastoral counselling are really not difficult and usually involve simple common sense. Perhaps the most important issue is that of confidentiality. If pastors wish for their parishioners to come to them and share the needs of their lives and relationships, they must learn to keep private information private. Without express permission from the counsellee, no information can be given out to others (including wives or husbands) without breaking this ethical rule. It is improper to even imply there is a problem (by asking others to pray, for example) unless permission has been granted and the counsellee is informed a prayer request will be made. It is certainly improper to use such information as a sermon illustration at any time without permission being granted. The appropriate time and place to share this information is in personal prayer time (alone) with God, who ultimately brings all healing and help in time of need.

This confidentiality usually extends to all information – with two possible exceptions. Those exceptions are child abuse (physical and sexual) and the commission of serious crimes. Some would say that even these are covered under the unique area of 'confessional information' given to a minister or priest. However, the laws governing such instances vary from country to country, and pastors should know the laws for the place in which they serve. Most countries now require that child abuse or even suspected child abuse be reported within 24 hours. At that point a person must search his or her conscience and perhaps seek the guidance of district and denominational leaders with experience.

A second ethical issue is secret keeping and message carrying in relational and family counselling. Because the purpose of counselling couples and families is to facilitate communication and truthfulness, secrets and secret bearing can be detrimental to the healing process. This is not to say that it is appropriate to break confidentiality in such cases. It is improper to share with another family member what one family member gives in confidence. A good strategy is to develop an understanding from the beginning that the goal of the counselling process is for the counsellees to share such information voluntarily and move the relationship forward.

In one situation, a husband informed the minister that he had made some 'business mistakes' that imperilled the family finances, and wanted to keep that information from his wife in hopes everything would resolve itself. The longer it went on, the more the husband found the pressure of the situation driving a wedge between himself and his wife, both emotionally and physically. On her part, the wife soon became afraid that because he was so distant and unavailable, he was having an affair, and she began to withhold herself from him. When she first used the word 'divorce', the minister realised how damaging the secret had become and pushed the husband to reveal the problem. He did. The wife was hurt and disappointed, but not to the extent of despair the imagined affair had created.

A word of caution may be necessary at this point. When counselling minor children, pastors must balance the need of the child to trust the counsellor with the need of the parents to know vital information. One counsellor shared that she would first seek the permission of the parents to treat information given by the children with confidentiality, with the exception that any necessary information important to the safety of the children would not be withheld. She would then tell the children that she would not tattle to the parents, but it would be necessary to give the parents some general information (not specifics of what the children might say) to reassure them of the children's wellbeing. She found most children and parents were comfortable with this formula.

A third ethical issue involves voyeurism. Most of what happens in the lives of others should remain within that private domain. There is such a thing as knowing too much, and such knowledge can ultimately drive a wedge between ministers and those they serve.

Finally, and hopefully most obvious, pastors should not become sexually or romantically involved with those they counsel. This may seem so obvious that it need not even be stated, but every year pastors are required to surrender their credentials, and their families are destroyed because they believed it could not happen to them. The compassion of a nurturing and caring pastor can be especially attractive to persons in vulnerable emotional situations. On the other side, positive emotional responses from counsellees can draw vulnerable pastors, who need the strokes because their own home life is less than positive, beyond compassion into an emotional (or even physical) relationship. Some simple rules can help prevent this from occurring.

- Do not counsel alone with individuals of the opposite sex. Let the professionals do this counselling.

- Counsellors should avoid sharing too much of their own private information with the counsellees. A good rule of thumb is to relate only that information that could be shared from the pulpit.

- Avoid counselling on sexual issues. Again, let a professional handle this.

Pastoral integrity can rarely survive where questions regarding moral and ethical reliability exist. In a profession where leadership is dependent on absolute trust, even innuendo can destroy the ability of pastors to shepherd effectively.

Liability. Are pastors legally liable for the counselling they engage in as ministers of the Church? The answer to this question is generally yes. This becomes especially true when they step outside their perceived area of expertise, which is spiritual counselling. Lawsuits involving relational (marriage and family) counselling and individual counselling have been brought against ministers and in some cases have been very successful. Litigation has become a way of life in this modern world, and it is too much to hope it will not invade the world of the Church and its servants. Many suggestions already given in previous paragraphs can help prevent liability issues from occurring. However, some additional suggestions may be helpful in either preventing or helping where liability becomes an issue.

Ministers should be acquainted with the law. Laws regarding the reporting of suspected (or proven) abuse or crimes are especially important. Much of this information can be obtained from the local office of social services, lawyers who specialise in liability issues, and other counselling professionals.

Counselling pastors should learn what ethical and moral guidelines they must follow in their counselling practice. Professional counselling associations, such as the Association of Christian Counsellors (ACC) have printed ethical guides for their members that can be helpful to pastors needing this information (see endnotes for contact information).

Joining a professional organisation such as the ACC, knowing their ethical standards and abiding by those standards in counselling situations, can often prevent liability problems and protect ministers in the event that charges of misconduct are made.

The old adage 'An ounce of prevention is worth a pound of cure' is excellent advice. Fear of liability issues should never deter pastors from giving the comfort their flocks need, but a good dose of carefulness and due consideration of appropriate conduct can prevent an early demise of their ministries.

In Conclusion

The responsibility of pastors to comfort and bring the healing process to bear on their parishioners' lives is at once a great privilege and responsibility. Ignoring proper protocol and careful practice in counselling can make that ministry more destructive than constructive. When done well and in a professional manner, it can be a vehicle for God to work great miracles. Again, the issue is not 'if' pastors will counsel but 'how' they will counsel. Whether they are gifted or whether for them it is a labour of love, all pastors should strive to do this ministry to the glory of God.

Notes

1. Edwin H. Friedman, *Generation to Generation: Family Process in Church and Synagogue* (New York: Guilford Press, 1999), 5–6.
2. David Dillon, *Short-Term Counseling: Utilizing Short-Term Therapy in Your Counseling Ministry* (Waco, Tex.: Word, 1992), 4.
3. James D. Hamilton, *The Minister as Marriage Counselor* (New York: Abingdon Press, 1961), 16.
4. Friedman, *Generation to Generation*, 7–8.
5. David G. Benner, *Strategic Pastoral Counseling: A Short-Term Structure Model* (Grand Rapids: Baker Book House, 1992), 27–28.
6. Everett L. Worthington Jr., *Marriage Counseling: A Christian Approach to Counseling Couples* (Downers Grove, Ill.: InterVarsity Press, 1989), 23–24.
7. Melvin Blanchette, 'Theological Foundations of Pastoral Counseling', in *Pastoral Counseling*, 2nd edn, ed. B. Estadt, M. Blanchette, and J. R. Compton (Englewood Cliffs, N.J.: Prentice Hall, 1991), 24–29.
8. David Olson and John DeFrain, *Marriage and the Family: Diversity and Strengths* (Mountain View, Calif.: Mayfield Publishing, 2000).
9. There are a number of books and informational sources available that give reliable information regarding what makes healthy individuals and families. See Conway and Conway, 2000; Olson and Olson, 2000; and Stinnet, 1999, in the bibliography.

10. Bill Blackburn, 'Pastors Who Counsel', in *Christian Counseling Ethics: A Handbook for Therapists, Pastors, and Counselors* (Downers Grove, Ill.: InterVarsity Press, 1991), 77.
11. Several books dealing with this method are listed in the bibliography.
12. Benner, *Strategic Pastoral Counseling*, 34–35.
13. Brad Johnson and William L. Johnson, *The Pastor's Guide to Psychological Disorders and Treatments* (New York: Haworth Pastoral Press, 2000), 135.
14. Blackburn, *Christian Counseling Ethics*, 80–81.

For Further Reading

Blackburn, Bill, 'Pastors Who Counsel'. In *Christian Counseling Ethics: A Handbook for Therapists, Pastors, and Counselors*. Downers Grove, Ill.: InterVarsity Press, 1991.

Blanchette, Melvin, 'Theological Foundations of Pastoral Counseling'. In *Pastoral Counseling*. 2nd edn. Edited by B. Estadt, M. Blanchette, and J. R. Compton. Englewood Cliffs, N.J.: Prentice Hall, 1991.

Benner, David G., *Strategic Pastoral Counseling: A Short-Term Structured Model*. Grand Rapids: Baker Book House, 1992.

Childs, Brian H., *Short-Term Counseling: A Guide*. Nashville: Abingdon Press, 1990.

Conway, Jim, and Sally, *Traits of a Lasting Marriage*. Wheaton, Ill.: Tyndale House Publishers, 2000.

Dillon, David, *Short-Term Counseling: Utilizing Short-Term Therapy in Your Counseling Ministry*. Waco, Tex.: Word, 1992.

Friedman, Edwin H., *Generation to Generation: Family Process in Church and Synagogue*. New York: Guilford Press, 1999.

Hamilton, James D., *The Minister as Marriage Counselor*. New York: Abingdon Press, 1961.

Henderson, D., 'Who Sees a Pastoral Counselor?' PhD diss., Loyola College, 1990.

Johnson, Brad, and William L. Johnson, *The Pastor's Guide to Psychological Disorders and Treatments*. New York: Haworth Pastoral Press, 2000.

Olson, David, and John DeFrain, *Marriage and the Family: Diversity and Strengths*. Mountain View, Calif.: Mayfield Publishing, 2000.

Olson, David H., and Amy K., *Empowering Couples: Building on Your Strengths*. 2nd edn. Minneapolis: Life Innovations, 2000.

Sanders, Randolph K., *Christian Counseling Ethics: A Handbook for Therapists, Pastors, and Counselors*. Downers Grove, Ill.: InterVarsity Press, 1997.

Stinnet, N., ed. *Fantastic Families: Six Proven Steps to Building a Strong Family*. West Monroe, La.: Howard Publishing, 1999.

Worthington, Everett L., Jr., *Marriage Counseling: A Christian Approach to Counseling Couples*. Downers Grove, Ill.: InterVarsity Press, 1989.

Wayne Schmidt, DMin, has served as a pastor at Kentwood Community Church near Grand Rapids, Michigan, since its inception in 1979. From a small care group it has grown to a vibrant congregation averaging over 2,500 in weekend worship services. Wayne has authored *Soul Management*, *Leading When God Is Moving*, and coauthored *Accountability: Becoming People of Integrity*. He and his wife, Jan, enjoy parenting their children: Chris, Jordan and Elsie.

The Leader's Planner
Striking the Balance

WAYNE SCHMIDT

There are many ironies in ministry. One is that we are sometimes called to speak the truth in an area where we have lived the lie. God demonstrates that indeed His strength is made perfect in weakness.

I'm a recovering workaholic. I lived the lie that a life out of balance somehow honours God. Now I'm writing a chapter on balance! This is a display of God's sense of humour – and a portrait of His grace. I have learned the lessons of balance the hard way, and I am enjoying the blessings of a more balanced life.

The Balancing Act – Realities
I've discovered that ministers visualise 'balance' in different ways. Some think of a balanced life as they would a balanced budget. There are certain categories in this 'balanced budget' (personal, family, professional, etc), and there are limited resources (24 hours in a day, 52 weeks in a year). Allotments are made in each category, as a reflection of needs and desires. Like a budget, when emergencies arise or desires are undisciplined, it no longer balances.

Other ministers visualise the balanced life as walking a gymnast's balance beam. A straight line is to be walked, and if a person loses his or her balance, heroic efforts are required to regain it. A little slip leads to a big fall.

Still others view balance as juggling. I have a friend who is a juggler, and while the result of his efforts appear magical, he assures me that juggling is nothing more than learning basic patterns and manoeuvres. It is a series of simple tasks that only seem complex. In this view of balance, if only the simple tasks are mastered, the 'magic' of the balanced life will appear.

There's the ever popular 'spinning plate' perspective. Here the minister must continually spin new plates and return to previous plates to give another spin. The spinner's investment of energy keeps previous plates spinning while he or she generates new initiatives.

Here is one more picture of balance. A well-balanced tyre on a car gives a smoother ride while avoiding unnecessary wear and tear. Like tyres, life requires its balance to be checked and adjusted.

These pictures of balance point to one reality. Balance is a moving target, not an ideal state. Leaders continually pursue balance because life is always throwing individuals off balance. Realigning life is a continual process, requiring self-reflection and self-discipline.

The Balancing Act – Roots

Self-reflection. Lack of balance in life can be driven by deeper motivations or states of soul – pride, insecurity, perfectionism, control. The lack of balance can be a symptom of other lacks in our lives. Imbalance is the fruit, but it's not the root. A person must stop and reflect to get to the roots.

The Root of Insecurity. As a recovering workaholic, I am now pained to realise that during my children's formative years, I was entirely too absent. My pattern of overcommitment to work persisted even though I attempted various external systems and constraints. Eventually it dawned on me that I was treating the symptoms, not the causes. The short-term result was that I suppressed those symptoms instead of digging to the root of the problem.

The root of my imbalance was personal and professional insecurity. I possessed a driving need to prove myself – to others, yes – but mostly to myself. I initially believed my passion for God and ministry was requiring all my time and energy. I now understand that my absorption in work was not because of God but was fuelled by my own sense of inadequacy. I felt valuable expending myself (and family) in ministry heroics, and worthless when I stopped running at full speed. I was becoming a human doing rather than a human being, and I was giving the most important relationships in my life only my emotional leftovers.

I had to experience a transformation, empowered by the love of God and others. In the words of Jesus, 'First clean the inside of the cup and dish, and then the outside also will be clean' (Matt. 23:26). Through devotional times in God's Word and prayer I built the conviction that my worth was found in being created in God's image and adopted as His child. I went to a few trusted friends and asked them to help me learn to build relationships that weren't just a by-product of doing something together but of simply being together. I used my personal journal to track my 'motive mixture'. I tried to discern how much of my life was truly a matter of giving God glory and how much was about relieving my false guilt. I asked God to enlarge my faith, and I acknowledged that He didn't require my imbalance to accomplish everything He desired through my ministry.

I'd like to say that my insecurity has been uprooted once and for all. Still today, years after consistently acting on my commitment to a balanced life, I sometimes feel as if I've 'lost my edge'. But what I'm finding far outweighs what I'm feeling. I'm finding joy in more intimate relationships. I'm leading a church that is even more effective in fulfilling its mission without being overly dependent on any one person. I have the privilege of mentoring others, providing an atmosphere where their gifts can flourish.

Insecurity was my 'taproot'. Webster defines the taproot as 'a root having a prominent central portion, growing vertically downward, and giving off small lateral roots in succession'. In conversations with others in ministry, I've discovered some other roots. I've identified my taproot and some of the lateral roots inside me. Let me encourage you to do the same.

The Root of Aimlessness. Many in ministry have never clearly defined their life purpose. Or if it was once clear, they have lost focus. The drift of life is not towards clarity but towards confusion. The question is, 'What is God's specific calling in my life?'

Good baseball batters don't courageously swing at every pitch. They are discerning – they know when to let a pitch go by and when to swing. They develop an eye for what is 'in the zone'. A clear sense of purpose provides a zone for life and ministry. By continually clarifying one's life calling, a person can discern when the expectations of others are legitimate, while refraining from activities and commitments outside the zone.

This process of determining what is on purpose gets more complex. When you play Little League baseball, you hit the ball off a tee, or a friendly coach pitches it to you. The higher the level of play, the more varied and difficult the pitches. The same is true in life. 'Whoever can be trusted with very little can also be trusted with much' (Luke 16:10). Good stewardship results in more opportunities, making the choices less obvious. No longer is it a matter of what is off purpose or on purpose but of what is most on purpose.

What is your clear calling as a believer? a spouse? a parent? a minister? What would it look like if you were living life completely on purpose?[1]

The Root of Independence. Ministers often have a built-in saboteur to balanced living. Their work involves a high level of independence. Few people in the congregation understand the demands of their leader's work or know what he or she is doing moment by moment. Daily tasks in the life of the congregational minister involve little imposed supervision or structure.

My grandfather worked in a factory. He had set hours, a specified task and an ever-present supervisor. His day was predictable and his daily agenda very tangible. As a minister, my hours vary greatly. I set my own schedule. Many ministers do, unless they are serving on a church staff where a supervisor provides structure. No one really knows how the minister spends his or her time. The minister sometimes does not know!

If you combine this schedule independence with a spirit of independence, a minister can face a rugged challenge. Many ministers leave the impression they 'answer only to God', conveying a 'how dare you ask' attitude. The root of the issue isn't nearly as spiritual. Numbers of leaders are unwilling to humbly answer to others and to invite individuals to ask about their use of time or about their priorities. A minister needs to set in place appropriate accountability, structure and boundaries. The schedule calls for it – and so does his or her spirit.

The Root of Rescuing. Several years ago Gordon McDonald, through his insightful book, *Restoring Your Spiritual Passion*, helped me see my relationship with people in a whole new way. While I highly recommend reading the book,[2] let me highlight the five types of people he identifies:

1. Very Resourceful People (VRPs) – they ignite our passion.
2. Very Important People (VIPs) – they share our passion.
3. Very Teachable People (VTPs) – they catch our passion.
4. Very Nice People (VNPs) – they enjoy our passion.
5. Very Draining People (VDPs) – they sap our passion.

Rarely do the VRPs and VIPs seek a great deal of our time. They usually have full lives and their own demanding schedules to manage. The further down the list you go, the more the people tend to come to the leader. By the time you get to the VDPs, their demands on a minister's time can be great. They seek their minister out – in the foyer, at the altar, by phone – they are there.

As ministers we serve the hurting, the broken, the needy. We all have times in our lives that require us to legitimately draw on the resources of others – to bear one another's burdens. Some people, however, are chronic VDPs. No matter how much the pastor does for them, it's never enough. If they are offered five minutes, they want 10; one hour, they want two.

The presence of VDPs in every church connects with a root in the life of many ministers – the need to rescue, to feel needed, to be the problem solver, the answer giver. Many ministers who avoid VRPs and VIPs because they stretch and challenge them spend unjustifiable amounts of time with VDPs because the role of the rescuer is more comfortable.

A minister may forfeit balance in life to make unreasonable investments of time and energy in the lives of people who will never consider that investment adequate. This imbalance created by the need to rescue others may precipitate a crisis at home, so he or she then may need to rescue his or her marriage or children. Often the rescuer ends up needing to be rescued. True compassion is rooted in the comfort of Christ, not the need to rescue.

Other Roots. I have witnessed other roots periodically in my own life and in the lives of other ministers. Some pastors seek to please people (give them what they want) rather than genuinely love people (give them what they really need). Some must have everything under control, requiring them to be omnipresent. Some are perfectionists, mistaking exhaustive effort for excellence.

What are some of the roots of imbalance in your life? Is there a taproot? What internal adjustments must be made to uproot these balance breakers from your soul?

The Balancing Act – Resources

Self-discipline. Once self-revelation uncovers the roots of imbalance, we're well on our way in our quest of balance. Next come the practical disciplines of managing life's roles and responsibilities. I've discovered that sustained self-management requires principle-centred living. These principles foster perseverance, the biblical basis of the character commitments required for a balanced life. Out of these principles arise the practices that maintain the balance or correct the imbalance.

Principles

1. 'No load.' According to Jeremiah 17:21–27, God instituted the Sabbath day as a day 'not to carry a load'. The principle of a day of rest goes all the way back to creation.

I place in my schedule one no load day a week, attempting to unplug from ministry both physically and mentally. I am not necessarily dormant on this day, but I'm not active in 'church business'. I may be contacted only in case of emergency. This forces me to equip others to carry out daily ministry responsibilities and makes the church less dependent on me. With a regular no load day, I'm capable of working smarter and more productively the other six days. Because my batteries are recharged on this day, I'm also more emotionally prepared to relate to my family and friends.

I also schedule a few no load days in a row at least once a quarter. This more extended release from the routine gives me a different perspective on all of life.

2. 'Saying yes means saying no.' Saying yes to a new responsibility or opportunity involves saying no to another responsibility or opportunity (unless I have unused capacity in my schedule, a rarity for those in ministry!). In 1 Corinthians 7:32–35, the apostle Paul emphasises that the person who marries has 'divided' his or her interests. When I chose to marry, I added a role to my life. When Jan and I became parents, another role was added. Each role rightfully reduced the commitment I could make to ministry. Often a minister mistakenly adds new commitments without reducing other commitments. With every new commitment ask, 'What must I now say no to, and is it God's will that I replace this commitment with another?'

3. 'Four gears.' In the book *Margin*[3] author Richard Swenson, MD, discusses living in four gears:

Overdrive – for life's excessive or unexpected demands.
Drive – in which we work and play.
Low – in which we develop deeper relationships with others.
Park – in which we develop our relationship with God.

Our culture, with its hurried pace, pushes us to live in drive and overdrive. While we're very active and productive, fewer people have healthy relationships and God seems distant. You cannot develop intimate, transparent relationships on the run. This is especially true of our relationship with God, who commands us to 'Be still, and know that I am God' (Psa. 46:10).

I've worked hard to resist the 'adrenaline addiction'[4] that moves me unnecessarily into overdrive. There are times that require high gear, but living in high gear breaks us down emotionally, physically and relationally. Try to build a little park and low into every day. The higher gears seem to happen without help. Holidays and days off should be lower gear times.

4. 'Rules are made to be broken.' We all carry an inward script of rules that whisper to us, 'If … then.' 'If I'm not always available, then I'm not a good pastor.' 'If I don't give my kids everything they want, then I'm not a good provider.' 'If I don't answer every request for denominational involvement,

then I'm not a team player.' 'If I take time out to exercise, I'm being selfish.' Many of these unwritten rules need to be challenged.

I talked recently to a friend in ministry who had stopped working out because he could not find a workout partner who needed to be evangelised or discipled. He felt blocking time for physical exercise alone was selfish yet realised his declining fitness was affecting other dimensions of his life. He was living with a rule that needed to be challenged.

If you make a new commitment or cease a previous one, ask, 'Is the "rule" that's guiding me a healthy or harmful one?'

5. 'Good enough.' I'm a believer in excellence, yet the cry for excellence has often become a cover for imbalance. The world celebrates one-dimensional excellence in athletics, music, and career. It makes heroes out of people who sacrifice everything for this unidimensional success.

The unexamined pursuit of excellence may feed a tendency towards perfectionism while undermining a capacity for balance. So I've developed a good enough perspective. For instance, in physical fitness I'll never run the Boston marathon. I do get an hour of exercise four days each week. I'm in good enough shape to maintain physical health and stewardship of my body.

6. 'Watch your battery.' Energy is the battery of life. Years ago I took the Personal Dynamic Profile (PDP). This diagnostic tool measures a person's types of energy and overall battery. I have a modest energy level – I run out of energy before I run out of hours in the day. I also discovered that while I have more than enough energy for starting something, I have little energy for sustaining what I've started! So a balanced life for me requires a more modest schedule than for some who have abundant energy. Since I don't have endless energy, I have to set my priorities even more carefully.

7. 'Life's a marathon.' Don't rust out by underutilising your abilities or burn out by overutilising them. I'm in marriage, parenting, friendships and ministry for the long run. Life is not a 100-metre sprint; it's a marathon. I want the emotional, physical and spiritual health to live a full life all the days God gives me on this earth. Determine your own rhythm[5] for living life to the full.

Practices

1. Clarify your specific purpose for each life area or role. Here's a sample listing:

Spiritual – intimacy with God, responding to His promptings
Personal – physically, emotionally, mentally
Family – marriage, children, extended family
Ministry – pastoral role, personal ministry opportunities

A specific purpose, or picture of health, for the spiritual dimension of your life might be, 'I have an intimate relationship with God that is fully integrated with every other dimension of my life, so that I am obedient to Him in all areas of living.' Create a similar purpose statement for each area of your life.

2. Identify those activities that support the fulfilment of your specific purpose in each life area. To achieve the picture of health described above, you may identify activities such as reading God's Word, journaling, praying, fasting, Scripture memory, listening to worship music, or reading devotional books. Once you've brainstormed a list, prioritise what you brainstormed, prioritise those you believe will make the greatest impact. The key is finding those that most help you personally, which John Ortberg identifies as the difference between 'training' and 'trying'.[6] Brainstorm a list of activities under each purpose statement you have created.

3. Work out a sample schedule including the activities needed to fulfil your purpose for each of your various life areas. Using possible activities in the spiritual dimension of life as an example, you may schedule half an hour each morning for Bible reading and prayer, a 'prayer walk' one hour each week, 10 minutes three days a week to write in a journal, and one hour each week to read a devotional book. Schedule activities in each life area.

4. Develop an accountability relationship with someone who will reinforce your resolve to incorporate each of these purpose-building activities into your life. In my book on accountability,[7] I describe the formation and key dimensions of an accountability partnership. My own accountability relationship has now lasted 17 years, and nothing has done more from a human perspective to help me pursue balance and overall wellbeing.

5. Track interruptions. Since the pastoral role requires flexibility and responsiveness to the unpredictable needs of people, I build some 'interrupt' time into every day of my schedule. If every moment is packed with preplanned activities, I view interruptions negatively. If I reserve some time for interruptions, I review interruptions carefully to determine their value.

I determine which settings result in a greater number of interruptions. For instance, when I am studying, I desire fewer interruptions, so I go to a local library. But on the day I schedule for interaction with other leaders in the church, my door is open and interruptions are expected and provided for in my schedule.

I also determine if there are certain people who consistently interrupt. I ask questions such as, 'Are their interruptions necessary?' 'Is this an indication that I need to schedule a regular time with them and then ask them to group their questions so we can address them at that time?'

I'm discovering that rooting out balance breakers, developing my life around balance-building principles, and at least annually going through the five practices is improving my balance.

Notes

1. Kevin W. McCarthy, *The On-Purpose Person* (Colorado Springs: Pinon Press, 1992). This wonderful 'parable' helps its readers discover both the value and methods of clarifying their purposes.
2. Gordon McDonald, *Restoring Your Spiritual Passion* (Nashville: Thomas Nelson Publishers, 1986). The author discusses these types of people on pages 71–91. His first book, *Ordering Your Private World,* is also valuable for developing convictions necessary for a balanced life.
3. Richard A. Swenson, *Margin: How to Create the Emotional, Physical, Financial, and Time Reserves You Need* (Colorado Springs: NavPress, 1992). The 'four graces' are discussed on pages 227–28. The author offers a doctor's perspective on balance and simplicity. A subsequent book, *The Overload Syndrome,* further develops his perspectives.
4. Archibald Hart, *The Hidden Link Between Adrenaline and Stress* (Nashville: Thomas Nelson, 1995). The author of this book is a psychologist. I believe one of the contributors to imbalance is the tendency for Type A personalities to produce adrenaline more often than needed.
5. Matthew Kelly, *The Rhythm of Life* (Steubenville, Ohio: Beacon Publishing, 1999). The author shares his own story of finding his rhythm for living and outlines a strategy for finding your personal rhythm.
6. John Ortberg, *The Life You've Always Wanted* (Grand Rapids: Zondervan, 1997). This book is an excellent resource on developing spiritual disciplines. In Chapter 3 the author distinguishes between trying harder and training.
7. Wayne Schmidt and Yvonne Prowant, *Accountability: Becoming People of Integrity* (Indianapolis: Wesley Press, 1991). This book was written in response to increasing numbers of requests from people asking how to choose an accountability partner and structure accountability goals and meetings.

Dale Galloway is dean of Asbury Theological Seminary's Beeson International Center for Biblical Preaching and Church Leadership. His history and heart have been in training pastors to be strong leaders. Through the four churches he pastored, two of which he started, he received international recognition as an innovative and visionary pacesetter, especially in small group ministry. During Dale's 23 years at New Hope Community Church, Portland, Oregon, the church grew to 6,400 members, 80 per cent of whom were previously unchurched. The need-meeting, pastoral-care-providing small groups reached 5,500 in total weekly attendance. Dale has authored 19 books including the two latest, *Building Teams in Ministry* and *On-Purpose Leadership*. He graduated from Olivet Nazarene University and Nazarene Theological Seminary, and was honoured with a doctorate from Western Evangelical Seminary. Dale and his wife, Margi, live in greater Lexington, Kentucky.

Implementing God's Vision for New Horizons

DALE E. GALLOWAY

A vision is the ability or God-given gift to see those things that have not yet become a reality. The Bible talks about vision in one of its definitions of faith: 'Now faith is being sure of what we hope for and certain of what we do not see' (Heb. 11:1). To paraphrase: 'Faith is vision, and vision is seeing it long before it is.'

Miraculous things happen when the leaders of a church get a clear-cut vision. Deep within, all of us have a need to make our lives count. There is nothing like an all-consuming vision to give our lives the meaning and purpose we long for.

Without a vision, life is humdrum and routine. The Bible says, 'Where there is no vision, the people perish' (Prov. 29:18, KJV). How true! But with a vision, life becomes exciting; and every day is a new adventure.

With a vision people not only tackle the impossible but also accomplish it. Without a vision, little worthwhile is ever attempted.

People without a vision can't survive long, and they definitely won't thrive. Vision adds excitement and enthusiasm to the lives of people. My heart aches for the scores of churches who view their ministries as boring 'business as usual'. Many people may love Jesus in those congregations, but they don't serve Him with enthusiasm.

The transporter of visions and dreams is the Holy Spirit. According to Acts 2:17, this new era is one where God says, 'I will pour out my Spirit on all people. Your sons and daughters will prophesy, your young men will see visions, your old men will dream dreams.'

As we learn to fellowship with the Holy Spirit, He acts as God's messenger, planting in our minds and hearts the seed thoughts of dreams and visions. When you live in the land of visions and dreams with God, life changes from ordinary to extraordinary. A day isn't just a day; each day becomes special.

Men and women of vision and dreams have no trouble praying because they have something to pray about. They have no trouble tithing, because they believe in it wholeheartedly. They have no trouble believing God for big things, because they know that God can do the impossible. They have no trouble with drifting and laziness, because they know where they're going and they're turned on for Jesus.

Our calling from God is to learn the life of the Spirit and to be people who respond to God's dreams. When we believe that 'nothing is impossible with God' (Luke 1:37), then we find ourselves setting measurable, realistic, motivating and attainable goals that challenge our faith.

What's needed today are people of vision who will see their church as a great supermarket eager to meet the complexity of needs that people face. The stronger a church becomes, the greater its impact in the community. The bigger its net, the more fish it can catch. The clearer a picture a church's leaders have of what God is calling and empowering it to do, the more those leaders will challenge, inspire and encourage the congregation to keep connected to God's vision and to keep moving to God's next levels.

Reaching Out to New Horizons

In the recent war against terrorism, launched after the gruesome attacks on the World Trade Center and the Pentagon, the United States maximised every resource available. High-speed computers searched the Internet worldwide to track the financial dealings and communications of the terrorist cells. B-2 stealth bombers took off from Missouri and dropped their load halfway around the world in Afghanistan. The United States president received the highest public approval ratings of any president in decades as he kept America focused on the goal – what we needed to do and why.

Without a goal, your life or mine becomes like an unplugged computer or an idle B-2 aircraft – having the potential to go anywhere but instead sitting still. What a waste of valuable resources it is to sit, day after day, going nowhere (or even being mediocre) when you could be reaching new horizons.

Years ago I was like a ship sitting at the dock, going absolutely nowhere. Life was at its lowest ebb, and it was all I could do just to make it through another day. It was hard enough to get out of bed; the thought of leading others forward seemed like a cruel joke.

With the help of God, I had somehow managed to stand back up after a devastating family crisis and all the ugly fallout at church. As I co-operated with God's work within me, wholeness began to replace my brokenness. I learned afresh that God specialises in giving dreams that ignite sparks of new life. I experienced God's promise that 'he who began a good work in you will carry it on to completion until the day of Christ Jesus' (Phil. 1:6).

God does the same with new vision for the next chapters in the life of a congregation. Even if a church knows nothing but a life of mediocre programmes and ho-hum spiritual passion, God can give you fresh vision, along with the wisdom of how to challenge the congregation to appropriate steps of faith.

Whether you're new at your church or just beginning a fresh chapter in a long-tenured ministry, God's future can be alive and growing inside you. He can empower your entire congregation to dream a new dream.

No matter what your ages, what circumstances your church has faced in the past or what has happened to you personally, you can dream a beautiful new dream. The fact that you're alive to read these words says that God is not finished with your life yet!

What would happen if your God-given imagination tried to visualise a pathway that would lead your congregation to new horizons? The process could be as simple as remembering these eight tools for setting your aim:

1. Prayerfully choose worthwhile goals. I once counselled a man who had a very clear goal – to steal his neighbour's wife. His goal was selfish and wrong. When he achieved it, he destroyed and devastated two families.

Most readers would not consider for a moment a goal as low as that, but we might settle for second best without realising it. One of my goal-setting problems in the past was that I didn't make love my No. 1 aim as the Bible teaches (see 1 Cor. 13:13–14:1). My first goal each day, my highest goal that makes my life so much more meaningful today than yesterday, is love. Love always wins.

As you establish goals in ministry, is it clear to all that the primary motivation behind your goals is love? In articulating a goal, I like to pray through three questions: Would this be a great thing for God? Would it help people who are hurting? And last in priority, would it bring out the best in me?

2. Tailor-make your goals. Most of us glean good ideas from other churches. If you've been stirred by some other church's mission statement or implementation goals, don't copy them point-blank. Find a realistic and appropriate adaptation for your context.

For example, the trend today is for new churches to start with a big splash – often with many months of building the core group and then several phases of 'grand opening' events. When my wife, Margi, and I started New Hope Community Church in Portland, Oregon, we had no money or backing. We didn't have the luxury of first building a large core group. So it would have been unwise for us to copy without adaptation someone else's first-year goals for attendance, finances or conversions.

3. Set your sights on something big enough to challenge the best in you. Time and again in the sports world, a No. 1 nationally ranked team has been knocked off by an unrated team. The experience challenges and stretches everyone involved.

I'd rather attempt something great for God and fail than to do nothing and succeed. Make your goals big enough to stretch your faith, bring out the best in your congregation and bring excitement to whatever you accomplish.

4. Stick with your goals. As a child, I had lots of fun with a magnifying glass. During hot summers in Columbus, Ohio, I'd go into the garden and examine everything I could. If I held the glass still and focused it on a pile of twigs, the power of the sun would focus, and to my boyhood merriment, I'd start a roaring fire. If I kept moving the magnifying glass from one place to another, I'd never achieve the desired results.

Suppose a couple said to you, 'Our goal is at some time to buy a house.' You would perhaps talk with them about sticking with their dream. You might also challenge them to be more specific. When will they buy? What price range are they seeking? What features do they want?

Likewise, churches often need to concentrate their focus. Too many churches go year after year unclear on what they're pursuing and not sticking to anything long enough to see it happen.

5. When setting your goal, don't focus on the obstacles. At each of the four churches I've pastored, God gave me a beautiful dream. At New Hope, for example, as I was reflecting on Jesus' ministry plan in Luke 4:18–19, God led me to the goal of building a ministry to reach unchurched thousands.

But in response I almost killed the church. I focused my eyes on the giant obstacles that scared me. They looked so impossible. I feared failure. Some of my friends told me I was doing something foolish.

Then one day I looked at Jesus, my Source of total supply, and I saw that with Him the impossible is possible. I fixed my sights on the goal, and at that moment, my entire frame of mind changed from negative to positive. I experienced the promise of God to be true once again: 'According to your faith will it be done to you' (Matt. 9:29).

As you set goals, don't attempt to overcome the obstacles before you start. Nobody would ever attempt anything of significance if all obstacles had to be removed before getting started.

I heard about a man who had to drive across town to get to work. He called the police station to inquire if all the lights would be green along the way. He had decided that if every light was green, then he would go to work. The dispatcher who answered hung up on him.

We laugh at the foolishness of that phone call, and yet how many times do we let a few red lights stop us from moving ahead? Just like this commuter, you reach your goal by taking one light at a time. After a while you overcome all the obstacles and arrive at your destination.

One of the things I've learned along the way is to wait on God's timing. If we don't get all the way to our goal this year, maybe next year will do it. If the obstacle doesn't seem to budge today, maybe next week God will give us a new resource or perspective to move the rock.

Expect some obstacles along the way. The greater your goal, the bigger your obstacles. Someone said, 'You measure the size of the accomplishment by the obstacles you must overcome to reach your goal.'

6. Break your large goal into small parts. When you eat, you do so one bite at a time, whether you're grabbing a small snack or sitting down to a smorgasbord or multicourse meal. Soon enough you can work through everything on your plate.

What would it look like for your church to accomplish a series of small wins on its way towards a large overall goal? What subgoals are bite-size enough for your congregation to accomplish. Maybe you can't feed all the homeless in your city, but can you do something to show the love of Christ to one family? to two families? to three families? Maybe you can't overcome all the hatred and prejudice in your town, but can your church build some specific, positive bridges of friendship with one group of people? with two groups? with three groups? Maybe you can't talk to everyone in your community about a faith relationship with Jesus Christ, but can your church reach 10 per cent more people than you did last year? 20 per cent? 30 per cent?

7. Deny the lesser to gain the greater. At different times in life I've faced the fact that I had allowed myself to become more than a stone overweight. Eating is a good thing; my problem comes from eating too much and not exercising enough. To lose my extra pounds, I have to deny the lesser (of eating) to gain the greater (being in good physical shape). The Bible tells us emphatically, 'To win the contest you must deny yourselves many things that would keep you from doing your best' (1 Cor. 9:25, TLB).

8. Set a date and get started. Someone said, 'Beginning is half done.' My preaching style has often been to write out my message. The most difficult part of the sermon for me to write is the introduction. When I finish it, I feel as if half the sermon is done, even though I've only just begun.

What is your church's next step (or first step) in getting started in implementing God's vision for new horizons?

Driven or Driving?

As you think about these vital components of vision, ask whether you and the church you serve are driven or driving. The answer will make quite a difference in your life and in the lives of those with whom you live and minister.

For too many years I was driven by my goals. This attitude resulted in tension in my life. Often I was insensitive and unresponsive to the needs of loved ones and co-workers around me.

It is a good feeling to have learned to set worthwhile goals and then be the master and manager of those goals, instead of becoming the slave to them. God gives great joy as I am learning to balance the ongoing stretch to new horizons while also enjoying each precious day to its fullest.

People who live in the Spirit of God are fun to be around. So are people who live in the spirit of God's next adventure. They are the ones who overcome their fears of failure with faith and, with God's help, reach beyond through the unknown to splendid new horizons.

At one of the churches I served, a lady made me a large green turtle. When she gave it to me, she pinned a note with these words: 'Behold the turtle. He makes progress only when he sticks his neck out.'

I am convinced that God put the turtle on the earth, if for nothing else, to teach you and me that unforgettable lesson. At one time or other, all of us fail, and the runaway feeling is to put our necks back into our shells and stay put. We're all tempted to play it safe.

You wouldn't be reading these words if God hadn't put the desire within you for something greater and the seed of faith to reach beyond to new horizons. To get there, you and the church you serve must step out of the shell of past failures. You need to stop licking your wounds.

So stick your neck out and begin to move ahead towards the vision and goals God has given you. There's no better time to start than now.

Seven Things to Do to Bring Your Vision to a Reality

1. Picture – get a clear-cut picture of the vision in your mind.
2. Heart – commit yourself to the fulfilment of the vision.
3. Soul – pray through until you know your vision is God's will for your life.
4. Focus – concentrate on the fulfilment of the vision.
5. Organisation – develop a master plan to accomplish the vision.
6. Risk – risk failure to gain success of your vision.
7. Faith – put into action your faith in the vision that God has given you.

For Further Reading

Barna, George, *The Power of Vision: How You Can Capture and Apply God's Vision for Your Ministry*. Ventura, Calif.: Regal Books, 1992.

Turning Vision into Action: Defining and Putting into Practice the Unique Vision God Has for Your Ministry. Ventura, Calif.: Regal Books, 1996.

Collins, Jim, *Good to Great: Why Some Companies Make the Leap ... and Others Don't*. New York: Harper-Collins, 2001.

Galloway, Dale, ed., *Leading with Vision*. Beeson Pastoral Series. Kansas City: Beacon Hill Press of Kansas City, 1999.

ed. *Making Church Relevant*. Beeson Pastoral Series. Kansas City: Beacon Hill Press of Kansas City, 2000.

ed. *Building Teams in Ministry*. Beeson Pastoral Series. Kansas City: Beacon Hill Press of Kansas City, 2001.

ed. *Leading in Times of Change*. Beeson Pastoral Series. Kansas City: Beacon Hill Press of Kansas City, 2001.

Galloway, Dale, with Warren Bird, *On-Purpose Leadership: Multiplying Your Ministry by Becoming a Leader of Leaders*. Kansas City: Beacon Hill Press of Kansas City, 2001.

Malphurs, Aubrey, *Developing a Vision for Ministry in the 21st Century*. Grand Rapids: Baker Books, 1996.

Stanley, Andy, *Visioneering*. Portland, Oreg.: Multnomah, 2001.

National Distributors

UK: (and countries not listed below)
CWR, Waverley Abbey House, Waverley Lane, Farnham, Surrey GU9 8EP.
Tel: (01252) 784700 Outside UK +44 1252 784700

AUSTRALIA: CMC Australasia, PO Box 519, Belmont, Victoria 3216.
Tel: (03) 5241 3288

CANADA: Cook Communications Ministries, PO Box 98, 55 Woodslee Avenue, Paris, Ontario.
Tel: 1800 263 2664

GHANA: Challenge Enterprises of Ghana, PO Box 5723, Accra.
Tel: (021) 222437/223249 Fax: (021) 226227

HONG KONG: Cross Communications Ltd, 1/F, 562A Nathan Road, Kowloon.
Tel: 2780 1188 Fax: 2770 6229

INDIA: Crystal Communications, 10-3-18/4/1, East Marredpalli, Secunderabad – 500026,
Andhra Pradesh.
Tel/Fax: (040) 27737145

KENYA: Keswick Books and Gifts Ltd, PO Box 10242, Nairobi.
Tel: (02) 331692/226047 Fax: (02) 728557

MALAYSIA: Salvation Book Centre (M) Sdn Bhd, 23 Jalan SS 2/64, 47300 Petaling Jaya, Selangor.
Tel: (03) 78766411/78766797 Fax: (03) 78757066/78756360

NEW ZEALAND: CMC Australasia, PO Box 36015, Lower Hutt.
Tel: 0800 449 408 Fax: 0800 449 049

NIGERIA: FBFM, Helen Baugh House, 96 St Finbarr's College Road, Akoka, Lagos.
Tel: (01) 7747429/4700218/825775/827264

PHILIPPINES: OMF Literature Inc, 776 Boni Avenue, Mandaluyong City.
Tel: (02) 531 2183 Fax: (02) 531 1960

SINGAPORE: Armour Publishing Pte Ltd, Block 203A Henderson Road,
11–06 Henderson Industrial Park, Singapore 159546.
Tel: 6 276 9976 Fax: 6 276 7564

SOUTH AFRICA: Struik Christian Books, 80 MacKenzie Street, PO Box 1144, Cape Town 8000.
Tel: (021) 462 4360 Fax: (021) 461 3612

SRI LANKA: Christombu Books, 27 Hospital Street, Colombo 1.
Tel: (01) 433142/328909

TANZANIA: CLC Christian Book Centre, PO Box 1384, Mkwepu Street, Dar es Salaam.
Tel/Fax (022) 2119439

ZIMBABWE: Word of Life Books, Shop 4, Memorial Building, 35 S Machel Avenue, Harare.
Tel: (04) 781305 Fax: (04) 774739

For email addresses, visit the CWR website: www.cwr.org.uk

CWR is a registered charity – number 294387

CWR's Online
Bookstore

Christian resources for everyday life and relationships

Offering a complete listing of all CWR's products, our Online Bookstore includes:

Our latest releases

A bargain basement

Forthcoming titles

Personalised pages

CWR CRUSADE FOR WORLD REVIVAL
Applying God's Word to everyday life and relationships

CWR'S ONLINE BOOKSTORE

www.cwrstore.org.uk

 CWR CRUSADE FOR WORLD REVIVAL — *Applying God's Word to everyday life and relationship*

The Leader's Guide to Effective Preaching

Written by 12 different church leaders, including Billy Graham and
Eugene Peterson, this is a book to encourage, challenge and teach
leaders/preachers how to develop and deliver messages that transform
lives. With each writer bringing his or her distinctive approach to this
book they include: the nature of expository preaching, communication issues in preaching and effective sermon planning – there is also
a chapter on the personal holiness of the preacher. This book is
designed to bring the preacher wisdom, sound thinking and practical
advice. The wealth of insights and counsel will help the reader to
grow and become a more effective leader/preacher.

£8.99 (plus p&p)

ISBN: 1-85345-323-4

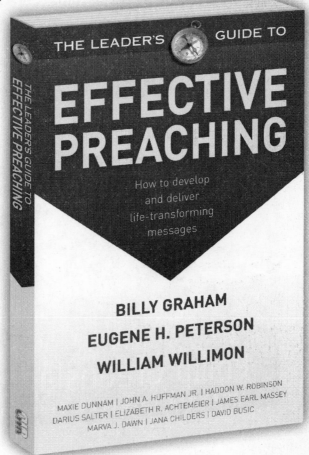

Leadership

An inspiring and challenging model for Christian leaders today.
Philip Greenslade takes us to the heart of the kind of leader
God is looking for.

£7.99 (plus p&p)

ISBN: 1-85345-202-5

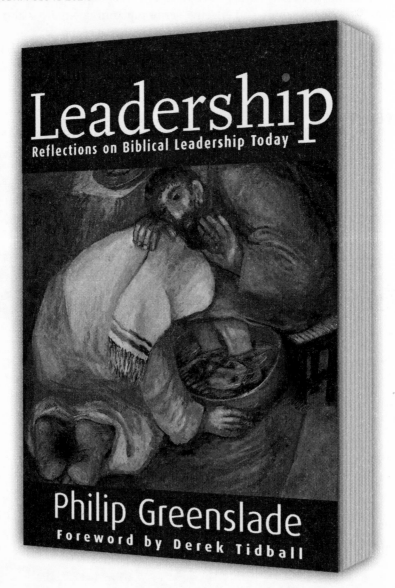

Pocket Encourager for Leaders

Biblical help, guidance and encouragement. This book explores
aspects of the Christian experience, such as relationships, Bible
study and coping with responsibility. This book is designed
to encourage and inspire leaders.

£3.99 (plus p&p)

ISBN: 1-85345-179-7